Education Reimagined

THE SCHOOLS OUR CHILDREN NEED

Ted Spear, Ph.D.

Eaglecliff Publishing

Cover Design: Kolton Babych

Education Reimagined/ Ted Spear. —1st ed.

ISBN: 978-1-9991744-0-8 (pbk)
ISBN: 978-1-9991744-1-5 (eBook)

Dedicated to Dyan Spear, my lifelong partner, who has continually offered unconditional love and encouragement as I have plunged headlong into sometimes dubious projects.

A gifted educator in her own right, she constantly reminds me to make the bridge between worthwhile aspirations and the realities that teachers and parents face every day. I have been fortunate to have had the benefit of her support and insight in everything I have done in my educational career.

ACKNOWLEDGMENTS

I am very grateful to the variety of people who read and commented on various versions of this book. These include Susan Alexander, Lois Belluk, Rick Brzezowski, Lesley Caves, Jeremy Church, Heather Coulthart, Meribeth Deen, Susanne Martin, Claire Maxwell, Susan Munroe, Don Plant, Julie Rogers, Eleanor Rosenberg, Paul Sweatman, and Ed Wachtman. Their suggestions and advice have made this a better book.

I am also incredibly lucky to have had communications expert Steve Mitchell take on the onerous task of editing this book. He was both thoughtful and appropriately unforgiving in the way he ploughed through my words with his weed wacker to help me get to the essence of what I wanted to say. If there are hiccups in the book, the fault is mine, not Steve's.

My thanks as well to Elizabeth Lyons, who guided me through the various mechanics of getting a book published, and who offered much-needed advice and encouragement along the way.

I am also fortunate to have been able to work with a remarkable group of teachers over the years at Mulgrave School in West Vancouver, Brookes Shawnigan Lake School on Vancouver Island, and Island Pacific School on Bowen Island. I have witnessed countless examples of their deep commitment and dedication to the students under their care. I have them in the back of my mind when I imagine what awesome teachers will look like in the next generation of schools.

Student: *Mr. Green, Mr. Green. Will this be on the test?*

Teacher: *Yes—about the test. This test will measure whether you are an informed, engaged, and productive citizen of the world. And it will take place in schools, and bars, and hospitals, and dorm rooms, and places of worship.*

You will be tested on first dates, in job interviews, while watching football, and while scrolling through your twitter feed.

The test will judge your ability to think about things other than celebrity marriages, whether you will be easily persuaded by empty political rhetoric, and whether you will be able to place your life and your community in a broader context.

The test will last your entire life, and it will be comprised of the millions of decisions that, when taken together, make your life yours.

And everything—everything—will be on it.

John Green
Crash Course History #1: The Agricultural Revolution (available on YouTube)

Contents

Preface

I have been a very lucky guy in my educational career. I got to do something that idealistic teachers and world-weary educational leaders can only dream of: I got to start my own school from the ground up.

While I will relate some of the ups and downs of that adventure in these pages, that's not what this book is about. Rather, it's about the lessons I learned along the way—from that school as well as others—and how they might be applied to the broader challenges of grade-school education as a whole.

There are two main audiences for this book. The first is parents. Perhaps you are a new parent beginning to explore the education options available to your infant or toddler when they reach school age. Or, maybe you are further down the road, already acting as a back-seat coach as your child makes his or her way through the school system.

For better or worse, that system will occupy and control a huge portion of your child's life. It will impose its cultural norms, rules, and expectations (or lack thereof) on twelve of their most formative years. It will provide either fertile or barren ground for their powerful, innate urges to discover and understand the world around them. It has the potential to be transformative, harmful, or irrelevant in the shaping of your child's life.

In this book I will propose that the job of grade school education is not simply to keep our kids off the streets or to prepare them for the world of work. Our purposes must be deeper than that—to equip and inspire students to cultivate their humanity. In the pages that follow, I will explain what I mean by this.

At the end of the day, it is all about the kinds of lives we want our kids to live. Will the thousands and thousands of hours they spend in grade school encourage them to pursue the richest and most profound picture of what their life might be? Or, will they simply represent a long sequence of bewildering tasks and hurdles that yield no ultimate meaning or impact beyond a set of letter grades or a GPA?

This book is for parents who want their child's grade school experience to be truly meaningful—who are curious about what that might actually look like—and want to know what they can do to help make it happen.

Specifically, it will give you the tools you need to assess and evaluate the educational options available for your child. It will provide an insider's perspective on when, why, and how to get involved as a parent at your child's school.

It will give pointers on how best to augment and enrich your child's education outside of the classroom. And it will show you how to be an effective advocate for better education with school administrators and elected officials.

The second intended audience for this book is teachers and educational leaders who know that something is not quite right with schools, but do not have the time or support to do things differently. What does this book offer you?

Simply put, it will help to untie your hands.

It will point the way to practical structural solutions that will allow you to follow your deepest intuitions about what you know to be central and important about grade school education. Hopefully, it will also inspire you to have the courage to break apart and reconfigure the very architecture of education to enable us to deliver on its true potential.

Several years ago, I attended a conference of educational leaders where we watched a brief video presentation by Benjamin Zander entitled "How to Give an A." The video proposed that we have invented a rather bizarre mechanism—grading—that creates and reinforces a destructive, and ultimately irrelevant, measure of student understanding and ability. I was not surprised when many of the senior educational leaders who were present concurred. They knew all too well how the distortions of grading can get in the way of a genuine education.

I was also not surprised, however, to see that their enthusiasm for considering any changes to the status quo was short-lived. Do you know what the kicker was? Their belief that *the parents would never go for it*. As much as they may have wanted, in their secret hearts, to radically reconfigure their schools to deliver on the dream of a truly transformative education, they felt their hands were tied to sticking with more conventional practices.

Educational change is coming; you can be sure of it. New technologies are driving a fundamental re-thinking of how education should be delivered and how schools should be structured and function. Certainly, with regard to educational practice, we are in the process of closing one chapter and on the cusp of writing yet another.

Given this great opportunity, we must not be deceived into adopting the trivial and banal. And we must not unthinkingly accept a new emerging status quo simply because it is new.

Our children and grandchildren face some of the biggest challenges humanity has ever seen. Climate change, the ubiquitous influence of social media, and the ever-increasing use of artificial intelligence and robotics are just a few obvious examples. Will our education system inspire and nurture the kind of vision, innovative thinking, and moral reckoning that this new world demands?

The challenge and responsibility for this generation is to have the courage to re-examine not only our approach to education but indeed our understanding of who we are and how we want to be as a species living on earth in the 21st century.

And by "this generation," I mean parents and educators together. We need parents who are prepared to accept and champion a deeper, richer education for their kids, and we need educators with the commitment to live up to this ideal.

More than ever, we need a partnership between parents and educators where everyone is "singing from the same hymn book" about the essential nature of the enterprise, while at the same time embracing the diversity of our kids and engineering the multiple pathways they will take to develop their better selves.

In thinking this over for the past couple of decades, it seems to me that it all comes down to different versions of love.

Parents love their children, plain and simple. They want the best for them, which usually means that they want them to be happy. I have three daughters of my own, and this is what I want for them.

Second, most teachers and educational leaders do, in fact, yearn for the deepest, richest, and most profound learning experiences for the children in their care. The profession of education is not something that most people pursue as a mere occupation; it is more like a calling, or—in other words—a particular expression of love.

Finally, there is something potentially magnificent about each generation creating a new social template about the way human beings should live and be on the planet. I say "potentially" because that template can be one of affirmation or destruction, hope or cynicism, hate or love. I am writing this book because I want this generation to choose love.

A Roadmap for this Book

This book offers general observations and aspirations regarding K-12 grade school education across North America. It does not attempt to deal with the enormous range of specific issues that arise in different educational jurisdictions across the continent. It examines, instead, a wide range of very practical concerns and challenges common to parents, teachers, and school administrators everywhere.

The central proposition of the book is that we need to fundamentally reimagine and then restructure K-12 education. This requires that we do two things:

- Commit to a deeper and richer core purpose of schooling: *to equip and inspire students to cultivate their humanity.*
- Have the courage to re-engineer the day-to-day structural elements of schooling in order to deliver on this purpose.

I will also propose that no such transformation can happen unless we can forge a mutually-supportive partnership between informed parents and inspired educators who share a commitment to a deeper, richer, and more powerful vision of what education can be.

To make this case, I am going to take us on a journey through eight way-stations:

Challenges & Opportunities: A brief overview of what is going wrong in contemporary education, what challenges we face, and why it is so difficult for us to change. Three reasons, nonetheless, to be optimistic about our opportunities to create remarkable schools.

Island Pacific School and Lessons Learned: A quick biographical sketch of why I started my own school, what that entailed, and some of the lessons that were learned along the way. Island Pacific School was my trial by fire that inspired me to imagine the larger possibilities within the broader educational landscape.

You Are Here: A brief historical survey that looks at the transition from the "Dominant" model of education to the current "Ascendant" model, with a critical look at a few recent initiatives. Also addressed: why we need a more substantial rendering of the next generation of schooling.

The Heart of the Matter: A clarion call to formulate a deeper, richer, and more powerful understanding of what we might accomplish within grade school education. A preview of the kinds of elements that might be included in such an education, followed by an invitation to pursue "deep prosperity" over individual self-interest as the touchstone of contemporary education.

Structure Matters: How re-engineering the structural elements of schools—class size and composition, schedules, instructional delivery, etc.—can help deliver much richer educational outcomes. Includes a new and likely controversial perspective on student assessment as well as some brief comments on educational finance.

Possible Futures: A review of innovations within several independent outlier schools, with associated commentary and cautions. Selected observations on what might be required to move forward, plus an example template for a high school program incorporating the elements proposed in the book, as well as a day in the life of a typical student attending such a school.

Pathways for Educators: Initial thoughts on how teachers and educational leaders might begin to adopt some of the ideas presented in the book, including a reality check on the potential scope of innovation. Brief sections on the importance of collaborating, communicating, and structuring for success.

Pathways for Parents: What parents can do at school and at home to orchestrate a quality education for their children. Proposes that parents can play a key role in improving schools by asking informed questions, being active partners, supporting intelligent innovations, and championing the public purpose of schools.

The book will conclude with a chapter that draws together these threads to reaffirm the proposition that with a strong partnership of parents and educators committed to a deeper vision of education and willing to make the necessary changes, we have a chance to make this next generation of schools reflect and encourage the very best of who we are.

Challenges & Opportunities

I have a friend who recently built a house and needed some beams made out of a large tree he had cut down on his property. On a whim, he contacted the woodshop of a local public high school and, to his surprise and delight, found that they were more than willing to do the job. It turned out that the Practical Arts teacher thought that his students should be exposed to precisely these kinds of experiences to gain a better appreciation of the craft. In other words, it was an individual educator committed to doing interesting things with his students that made this happen.

Over my thirty plus years of experience in public and independent schools, I have seen countless such examples of remarkable teaching and engaged learning. In every case, it has been individual teachers and educational leaders who have taken personal initiative to make something worthwhile happen for kids.

I have also seen my fair share of uninspired instruction and unbearable tedium on the part of students and teachers alike. Almost all those instances have been made at the implicit invitation of the system as a whole.

Most of the really great things that happen in schools come about when individual teachers or learning assistants decide to put their own personal stamp on a program or process, sometimes—perhaps often?—quite outside the regular operational parameters of the institution. Much of the uninspired teaching and unbearable tedium, on the other hand, comes about when there is no motivation and support to do otherwise. One of our biggest challenges, therefore, is to give individual practitioners both the reasons and the structural support they need to do remarkable things with their students.

THE HIGHER YOU GO, THE WORSE IT GETS

Here's a familiar yet interesting phenomenon in K-12 education. Kids in elementary schools are generally naturally inquisitive and willing to explore all kinds of possibilities. They are like sponges soaking up massive amounts of external information. It is remarkable just how much they are able to take in. Middle school students, on the other hand, often flatline in terms of their intellectual curiosity, as their attention shifts to interpersonal interactions or external preoccupations: sports, social media, computer games, etc. At Island Pacific School—as I will explain later—we found that we needed to make it an explicit goal to sustain and enhance intellectual curiosity and creativity during these years.

High school is a different story. The internal interest and engagement that students carried with them through the elementary and (hopefully) middle school years is replaced with an external obligation to grind through the courses and meet the requirements of graduation. Because high school students become habituated to the acceptable ways of school "learning," they dutifully do what is required of them, but it often has little meaning in their lives.

I once had a very inspired math teacher who loved to take her students on wildly imaginative intellectual adventures illustrating the beauty and complexity of math. Much of what she did was not part of the prescribed curriculum. When students moved out of our middle school into high school, we occasionally got back in touch with them to see how things were going. I remember one student who actually "dropped down" and struggled in grade 10 and grade 11 math after leaving our school. She eventually managed to claw her way back up the assessment scale by the time she completed grade 12. When I asked her about this, I will never forget her response. She said that, although she was eventually able to "do well" on her math courses, she "didn't like math anymore."

She is not alone. Results from a student satisfaction survey conducted by the British Columbia Ministry of Education[1] indicate a steady decline in favourable responses—from elementary school to high school—regarding student perceptions of school.

Students Reporting "Many Times" or "All the Time" to the Question: Do You Like School?

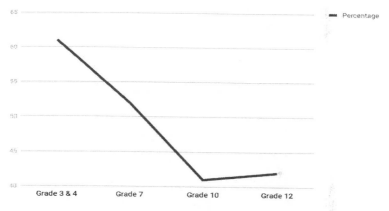

BC Ministry of Education: 2015-16 Academic Year

Students Reporting "Many Times" or "All the Time" to the Questions:
Do you like what you are learning at school? (Grades 3 & 4, 7)
Are you satisfied with what you are learning at school? (Grades 10, 12)

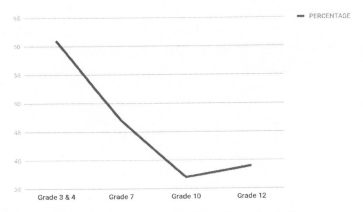

BC Ministry of Education: 2015-16 Academic Year

The experience in British Columbia is no different from many other jurisdictions. Respected educational author and consultant Michael Fullan points out that "Studies from many countries show that among high school students less than 40% of upper secondary students are intellectually engaged."[2]

Theoretically, we should not see a decline in interest and engagement as students progress through grade school. As we build their capacity through the years and introduce them to broader vistas, they should, in fact, become *more* interested and engaged by the time the get to high school.

Part of the reason that this is not the case might be revealed in another BC survey statistic: only 32% of high school students report that they have many "opportunities to work on things [they] are interested in as part of [their] coursework."[3] It is unlikely that many other educational jurisdictions would fare much better.

It took a comment by a grade 11 student to really bring the problem home for me. He was giving a public presentation of a film he had created about his dad's triumph over a brain tumour operation. As this was a school-sponsored project, he fit into the 32% of students who actually got the opportunity to work on something of personal interest. It was a profound and moving piece in which he was completely invested—technically, artistically, and emotionally. In other words, a perfect educational experience. That said, in the course of questions from the audience about how he managed to find the time to create such a remarkable film amidst his regular school studies, he quipped, "It's crazy how much school slows you down in what you want to do." He has since gone on to become a brilliant photographer who has parlayed his fan base of over 200,000 followers into lucrative photography contracts that take him all around the world.

The core challenge here is that if we do not actively and intentionally create opportunities for kids to discover and then develop their interests, abilities, and passions—particularly in the senior years—we squander their talents. In doing so, we significantly reduce their chances of finding joy, success, and meaning in their lives and deny ourselves the very real contributions they could make to society.

The reality is that many high school graduates have little idea what they are interested in, for the simple reason that identifying potential passions and then developing them into full-blown capacities has never been a driving force of schools. Many of them elect the default choice of attending college or university—if they can get in—because this is what "everyone" does. Their decisions about which institution to attend are often not derived from a burning passion to pursue a field of study, but rather based on parents' expectations, the consideration of where friends are going, or which city seems most appealing. Similarly, their selection of courses is frequently lacking in focus or direction with the vague hope that some interest or sense of purpose might emerge at some point further down the line. Meanwhile, those who don't get accepted into colleges and universities gravitate to whatever job they can get. In either case, developed ability founded on personal interest is rarely part of the equation.

This is the exact opposite of the way things should be. By the time our students graduate high school, they should be both able and inspired to passionately pursue interests that ring true for them. If we create an education system that doesn't set them up to do this, we do a grave disservice not only to our students but also to our collective future.

HUMANITY ERODED

We have another challenge to consider as well. There is something else missing in grade school education, and it goes beyond the creation of opportunities for young people to discover and develop their interests and abilities.

How many times have you witnessed, or entered into, argumentative exchanges that quickly lapse into incoherent distortions of the issues and principles at hand? How many times have you encountered people who are simply incapable of following a line of reasoning to its end or, more to the point, are willfully uninterested in doing so?

A year or so ago I happened to listen to a radio talk show program wherein the participants were discussing the proposed introduction of special rent rules for homeowners in Vancouver to help the city deal with a critical lack of affordable housing, which was creating chronic hardship for thousands of individuals and families as well as long-term problems for the viability of the city. Listeners were invited to call in with their opinions. I will never forget the final comment of one such contributor. "Homeowners should be allowed to charge whatever rent they want. If you can't afford a home, how is that my problem and why it that my problem?"

There it is: a complete incapacity, or intentional lack of interest, to see something from the other person's point of view. A succinct encapsulation of the modern triumph of individual entitlement over the kind of shared understanding that might lead to compassion.

Over the centuries, human beings have worked hard to develop certain kinds of understanding and certain gifts. As the result of sometimes horrific experiences, we have acquired the wisdom to understand the sources of our pain and suffering. We have also acquired the powers to reason, to explore, to be creative, to be moral agents, and to wonder at our place within narratives that are bigger than ourselves. These are hard won gifts that should not be squandered but instead be used and improved upon.

These are, moreover, public goods because when they are distributed broadly across our population, they enrich not only the individuals involved but society as a whole. They make us, collectively, more just, curious, vibrant, wise, and—ultimately—compassionate.

I see K-12 education as the best place to expose young people to these gifts—to introduce them to human achievements, to teach them about reasoning, and indeed to provide the foundation for compassionate understanding. But schools, at present, do not frame their purposes in this way. It is time they did.

THE CHANGES WE CHOOSE

The world beyond education is changing rapidly. A now dated YouTube video entitled Humans Need Not Apply shows all too clearly the way that much of the work we currently do—notably in white collar occupations—will be replaced by automation. Legal research and medical diagnoses can now be done more quickly by computers than persons. Rapid advances in artificial intelligence are accelerating these trends.

How do we prepare coming generations for a future we are unable to predict? The educational changes we make can't simply aim at teaching students the discrete skill sets we imagine they will need for the emerging new economy by, for example, teaching everyone coding. That is a guessing game we are sure to lose.

Instead, the solution is to find and develop those more fundamental human capacities that will enable the next generation to deal with challenges and opportunities that we can't even envision. In a rapidly-changing world, we are going to need our citizenry to drink from a deeper well than one that offers a simple set of occupational skills at the expense of wisdom, compassion, and understanding.

What we are really looking for, in fact, is the kind of education for our sons and daughters that seeks out and celebrates their distinctive interests and abilities in a way that connects them with a larger human narrative. We do not want our kids to simply survive within the world as it is—we want them to embrace the world as it could be.

WHITHER PUBLIC EDUCATION?

I started my own independent school because I was impatient with what I believed to be the shortcomings of the contemporary system. I have not been alone. Even though 90% of all students currently attend public schools, enrollment in private and independent schools is ever-increasing[4], while funding to public education continually declines.[5]

Is that a good thing? I don't think so.

Although I enjoyed the luxury—and accepted the considerable challenges—of operating my own school, I know that our reach was limited. While I think private and independent schools have their own important contributions to make, it is going to be the way we manage our public schools—where the vast majority of society receives basic education—that will make the decisive difference to our future.

OVERCOMING INERTIA

Most of us find it very difficult to imagine a completely different way of looking at something than what is thoroughly embedded within our memories and everyday experiences.

A good friend of mine once quipped that "fish discover water last." What he meant was that, once immersed within a particular set of assumptions, expectations, and experiences, it is difficult—if not impossible—to break free of those. It is also impossible to see that one's "world" is, in fact, only a fish bowl.

I often ask young parents what they want for their children in school. More often than not, they instinctively gravitate toward some version of "water" in a familiar version of a "fishbowl." Some say, for example, that they want their kids to be conversant with "technology," but they are vague about what exactly they mean by this. Almost all of them implicitly assume that schools will remain more or less as they are now. We are so immersed in the predispositions of the status quo—even the emerging status quo—that we are incapable of asking the more fundamental question: what might education really be for?

Curiously, even though many of us might acknowledge the limitations and inadequacy of the existing grade school experience, we seem to be willing to accept this status quo with a simple shrug. The inevitability of high school, in particular, being an imperfect but necessary burden to be endured is deeply embedded in our cultural mindset.

Quite a few years ago, I owned a beater of a car that got lousy gas mileage, gave off noxious fumes, couldn't get up big hills, had window wipers that wouldn't wipe, and was cursed with an alarm that went off for no discernible reason. I knew all of this, and yet I could not bring myself to think about replacing my car, let alone re-imagining my whole approach to personal transportation.

I think this is more or less how we think about K-12 education today. Some of us know that its operating range is limited, that parts of it do not work, and that it can actually be damaging to some of those within it, yet we can't bring ourselves to "replace the vehicle." We seem to be incapable of rethinking what we are trying to accomplish in schools and then reimagining better ways to deliver on our purposes. When we change at all, we tinker. We install a fancy new GPS monitor on the front windshield and take pride in our capacity to embrace innovation.

Perhaps the biggest challenge we face, therefore, is to get beyond the inertia of simply replicating the past or constructing a future that once again
aims too low in its estimation of the true potential of education.

A POSSIBLE DISCONNECT

In this book, I am going to challenge fundamental assumptions about grade
school education: its purpose, content, structure, personnel, and funding. I
am going to do this because—irrespective of the many beautiful and heroic
things that happen in public and independent schools—I am convinced that
our overall approach to education is selling our children short. I will make
this case, however, with some admitted fear and trepidation about being
fundamentally misunderstood.

Here's the thing: most teachers and educational leaders in public and independent schools approach their work from a place of goodwill; they genuinely want the best for their students, and they typically work very, very
hard to ensure that students get what they need. Their manifest purpose—
their intention—is to do right by their students.

I have a good friend who is a public school elementary teacher. She goes
into work every day with a predisposition to do the best she can for each
and every student in her class. In many ways, she is successful in this regard,
for she is particularly gifted at nurturing one-to-one relationships with students while directing the ebb and flow of the class as a whole. Although she
is justifiably proud of the connections she has been able to make with her
students, she nonetheless frequently comes home at the end of the day
completely exhausted by the professional and emotional demands of her
job. And yet, she nonetheless sometimes has misgivings about "not being
able to do enough" for the children in her care.

There are thousands of people like my friend out there—teachers who
strive mightily to do the best for their kids but operate in an environment

that is functionally incapable of giving students a truly rich education. I think there are a couple of reasons for this.

First, we seem to take for granted, and therefore sidestep, the fundamental question of the core purpose—and potential—of education. We accept the implicit assumption that schools are likely doing something reasonably worthwhile with students, even if we are not always sure what that might be.

Second, this lack of vigilance about core purpose means that the structural elements in our current system—for example, the way we group and arrange classes, the way we "deliver" curriculum, and the way we manage assessment—actually come to define and ultimately limit our approach to education.

My point is this: even though we walk into our classrooms with the best intentions, the way we understand and structure our schools creates unintended or unanticipated effects that restrict us from realizing the full potential of education.

OPPORTUNITY BECKONS

While the challenges to fundamentally reimagine grade school education are significant, there are three good reasons why the time is ripe to change our approach to schooling.

First, we are already witnessing a changing of the guard regarding our techniques (though not necessarily our purposes) of instructional delivery. From the 1960s onward, there have been countless critiques of the "factory-school" model of education, which emphasized standardized delivery of prescribed content in favour of a more "student-centered" approach. That critique is now, more or less, coming home to roost. There is, for example, a big emphasis these days on what is called "personalized learning." While we are indeed well rid of many elements of the factory-school model, and while certain elements within the emerging model indeed have promise, we need to be careful that we do not replace one system of education with another that is equally insufficient. The immediate point, however, is that in this changing of the guard, there is now an *opening* to re-examine what we are doing in education and why.

Second, emerging technologies do provide the opportunity to bring about significant changes in education, but not necessarily in the ways we might initially imagine. For the first time ever, we might be close to solving the central problem of so-called personalized education: the challenge of creating an infrastructure that would enable all students—not just the minority in specialized programs—to gain an education that would provide them with a strong foundation from which to discover and develop their own interests, abilities, and passions. Technology is going to be the lever (but not the driver) that will help us to meet one of our most cherished goals.

Finally, we have a new generation of educators who are incredibly keen to build a deeper, richer, and more worthwhile version of what schools can be. The inspired teachers and older alumni students I talk to are all after the same thing: the desire to make a positive contribution in the world through the full expression of their abilities. I see an infinite reservoir of commitment and goodwill just waiting to be tapped.

If we are able to act on these opportunities, the future of K-12 education is indeed promising. Imagine, for example, what it would be like to go to a high school where students:

- are given essential tools (basic grammar, etc.) and pre-requisite soft skills (working in groups, etc.) that enable them to get the most out of a program that demands personal engagement and competence.

- are introduced to subject matter in a way that connects the dots to reveal a "great conversation" of human inquiry, rather than a list of discrete factoids to be memorized and forgotten.

- are expected to pursue questions and projects of personal interest in a way that does not compete with but instead constitutes a good portion of their formal program.

- are confronted with a set of carefully crafted personal challenges that are designed to bring about a strong sense of *warranted* confidence within them.

- are required to temporarily remove themselves from their immediate social or cultural experience in order to see things from a different perspective.

- are explicitly invited to self-cultivate those qualities of character necessary for the fullest expression of the very best of what it is to be a human being.

Further, imagine having students graduate from this school with such a strong sense of their interests and abilities that they are eager to launch into the next chapter of their learning journey. All of this is possible; in fact, some of it is already happening. The opportunity beckons to bring this model to scale for the benefit of all students.

I have become passionate about the potential for grade school education partially as a result of my graduate studies but most importantly through three decades of learning with students and teachers. In addition to working in various public and independent schools, I had the opportunity to create my own school from the ground up. It has been a long road from there to here, with plenty of mistakes, lessons, and insights along the way. A brief review of this journey will help to explain some of the observations that follow.

Island Pacific School: Lessons Learned

What Possessed Me?

In 1995, a few parents, community volunteers, and I started a small grade 7-9 middle school in British Columbia, Canada. We called it Island Pacific School (IPS), in part because it was located on an island 20 minutes by ferry from Vancouver.

What possessed me?

I think it was somewhere around my second year of university when I first got it into my head that I wanted to start a school. I was becoming increasingly frustrated and unimpressed by the educational terrain I had encountered, as well as what seemed to lie in the future. I was, for better or worse, bitten by the bug early on to create something new and unique in grade school education.

I suspect that one source of my initial motivation was a somewhat bizarre and infamous school that I attended in my own adolescent years. When I was thirteen, my parents sent me to a school named St. John's Cathedral Boys' School, which was located about forty kilometers north of my hometown of Winnipeg, Manitoba. If you Google St. John's, the stories that stand out are the ones about the outdoor tragedies the school has faced[1] and the case of the teacher who sexually assaulted several students during the 1982-83 school year.[2] Thankfully, I attended the school long before any of that happened. I was there, however, when the school sent boys on arduous canoe and snowshoeing trips (I completed two epic canoe trips and a one-day, 50-kilometer snowshoe race) and the teachers employed corporal punishment to either "motivate" students to learn or enforce rules. We would receive swats across the rear if we performed poorly on math tests, were caught speaking after lights out, or did not complete our regular clean-up duties to their satisfaction. A maximum of ten swats was awarded to anyone who smoked or ran away.

My parents were apparently worried that I lacked drive, so they figured the St. John's environment would do me some good. Although St. Johns wasn't a reform school in the traditional sense of that word, it was a pretty rough place attended by some interesting characters. It was a jeans and T-shirts school, not a setting for ties and blazers. And it was, back then, a place where "new boys" were hazed, i.e., required to clean the dorms of older boys and given inventive punishments when their work was inevitably not up to standard.

After my first year in grade eight at St. John's, I asked my parents to pull me from the school, and they agreed. But then, an interesting thing happened. I returned to my suburban junior high school and was surprised to find it, by comparison, both mundane and unremarkable. So, I asked my parents to send me back to St. John's for grade 10, which they did.

Why did I return? In hindsight, I think I sensed that St. John's was an authentic community in the midst of an often-inauthentic world. The teachers who taught there were all voluntary members of an Anglican association called the Company of the Cross. During my time there, they were given room and board and paid, incredibly enough, a dollar a day. These people were committed. The founding heads, Frank Wiens and Ted Byfield, had a vision of education that they were absolutely tenacious in promoting. I remember the Sunday evening chaplain services in which Frank Wiens would occasionally offer advice about what it would look like to live a good life. Although I did not always agree with everything he said, I remember being impressed by the fact that he said these things—that he made a point of talking to boys about the very meaning of life.

Looking back on my own experience at St. John's—quite apart from any consideration of its subsequent tragedies—I am of two minds about its ultimate legacy as an educational experiment. On one hand, it's clear that its use of corporal punishment and its complicit failure to disallow hazing are attributes of older educational institutions that are best left far behind. On the other hand, there was something compelling about telling young men, in no uncertain terms, that they had to take responsibility for themselves and be mindful and intentional about how they conducted themselves in the world.

I left St. John's after my grade ten year, after having survived snowshoe practices, canoe trips, and the occasional swat with the knowledge that I had experienced something unmediated and very real. Unlike so many other sensations and experiences in my life to that point, this one made an impression.

Other early points of reference for some of my subsequent thoughts on education included volunteer work with preteens and mentally challenged young adults, and summers spent as a camp counsellor and wilderness canoe trip leader. In looking back at these years, I realize that I was given the opportunity to take significant responsibility for others at a relatively young age. What I have understood ever since is the deep capacity that young people have to accept this kind of responsibility, and the importance of making sure they get the opportunity to do so.

My own life as a teenager and young adult likely predisposed me to emphasize education as a nurturing ground for character. It was not until graduate school, however, that I began to think a bit more deeply about the importance of substantive content.

I remember in my third year of graduate school coming to the stark realization that I was not, in fact, particularly well-educated. At that time, I was trying to put together a doctorate in philosophy of education, and I was struck, over and over again, by how ill-equipped I was to write and think in any coherent form, and how breathtakingly ignorant I was about so many things in the world.

I had, until that point, lived happily with the conceit that because I graduated from high school and completed a master's degree, I was reasonably knowledgeable. However, what I eventually came to realize in my doctoral program was that there were whole oceans of knowledge and understanding that I had not even dipped my toes into. What also struck me as unforgivable was that it should not have taken me until graduate school to come across the ideas I was encountering.

For example, I remember stumbling across Karl Popper's proposition that what distinguishes scientific claims from non-scientific claims is the principle of falsifiability, i.e., the idea that scientific claims are intentionally structured in a way that they can be shown to be wrong. If I claim that water boils at 100 degrees centigrade at sea level, then an instance of water boiling at 105 degrees invalidates that claim. Non-scientific claims, on the other hand, are subject to no such rigor. If I claim that you will meet a tall dark stranger on Tuesday if the stars align accordingly, and you do not meet a tall dark stranger (because, after the fact, the stars apparently did not align accordingly), then I have not set up a condition that can be falsified.

Now, this idea, in and of itself, is not very difficult to grasp. It is the kind of thing that should be presented to students in middle school. While there is, to be sure, plenty of learned debate about the applicability of Popper's principle to science as it is practiced at the quantum level, for example, his idea is nonetheless an excellent starting point to an ongoing conversation with students about what science might actually be. And it is most certainly a conversation that should not wait until graduate school.

As it has been with Karl Popper's principle of falsifiability, so too has it been with so many other things: the patterns explicit within mathematics, the underlying structure of arguments, the genius of poetry, the bounty of history. All of these things had been withheld from me to be revealed, often by accident, through independent study. And all of them have come to me at a time far beyond what might have been optimal in terms of building a deep appreciation of the subject.

I still remember the shock of realizing that I had not received an education, in any deep and rich sense of that word, but instead a kind of cheap facsimile wherein I had dutifully attended school, completed myriad assignments and tests, and walked out breathtakingly ignorant about so many basic things. I also remember thinking that at least two whole generations had been fed the same fare. It was this realization, perhaps more than any other, that made me determined to try to formulate something deeper, richer, and better for the next generation.

Fortunately, in graduate school, I also had the opportunity to be exposed to the history of education and the many alternatives that have been championed in the past. I remember being inspired by the fact that there were other powerful models and possibilities to consider, and we did not necessarily have to settle for something that was ill-conceived or substandard.

My teaching and administrative experience in the field more or less confirmed my reservations about grade-school education. I taught in the public system at a First Nations reserve school in Northern Manitoba and at a high school in Haida Gwaii. I also worked at an independent college in Vancouver that catered mostly to international students. Later on, during a four-year "sabbatical" from Island Pacific School, I served as a middle school principal at a prestigious independent school in Vancouver, and then went on to co-found another independent grade 7-12 school on Vancouver Island. While all of these places had their fair share of committed teachers and administrators, I could not shake the feeling that it was the system as a whole that was letting the students down.

The school on Haida Gwaii was an interesting place in that it was meant to serve three different populations of students: First Nations kids, the children of military families working at a (now closed) military installation, and the offspring of back-to-the-landers who had moved to the islands a generation earlier to get away from contemporary society.

As a teacher, I was expected to perform my standard teacher repertoire: walk my students through various units, assignments and tests, and create various report cards to record their respective levels of "achievement." I think many of us knew, however, that much of this was a hollow exercise that had everything to do with classifying and accrediting students and very little to do with creating the conditions to allow them to develop as persons.

I remember being particularly worried that we were not doing a good job of meeting the needs of one of our constituent populations, namely the First Nations kids. There wasn't much connection between the curriculum we were teaching them and the lives they actually lived. What I eventually came to realize, however, is that our school—purposed and structured as it was— did not do a good job of serving *any* population particularly well. The entire philosophical and operational architecture was at fault. It was finally time for me to try something different.

Island Pacific School: Lessons Learned

Starting a School from Scratch

Have you ever had an idea about something and all prudent analysis would seem to indicate that it is a bad idea and it won't work? In the case of Island Pacific School, that analysis turned out to be initially right and then spectacularly wrong.

The problem was that I got it into my head to start a school on a very small island. After completing my doctorate degree and working for a few years at an international college in Vancouver, my young family and I moved to Bowen Island, which is a 20-minute ferry ride from Horseshoe Bay in West Vancouver. While Bowen Island turned out to be a beautiful place to raise our three daughters, it was not initially the most intelligent place to start a school. The total population of the island was about 3,200 in 1995 when we started and still had only 3,700 permanent residents as of the 2016 census. If we had founded the school in Vancouver, it likely would have been triple the size or more by now. At present, Island Pacific School enrolls between 60-70 students in grades 6-9, which works out to one class of 15-18 students at each grade level.

As it turned out, however, the school's small size and relatively slow growth over time turned out to be its saving grace. Unbeknownst to us, we had given ourselves the luxury (and hard work) of building an educational infrastructure piece by piece from the ground up on a schedule that gave us time to reflect on and correct our mistakes.

We began in 1995 with a mix of fourteen students in grades seven to nine. I laugh when I think back on it. I held the first summer meeting with our new staff—part-time science, math, and French teachers—in the basement of our home because we did not yet have a building. (A building materialized in September in the form of a rental property purpose-built by a local supporter.) When classes began, we ran a kind of three-ring circus in a single classroom that artfully segregated and blended the curricula for each grade level.

The underlying proposition of Island Pacific School has always been that the middle years are an incredibly important transition period that we need to get right. We knew that these years can be a time where kids flatline in terms of their intellectual curiosity and a time where young people can choose to accept the multitudinous "invitations to stupidity" that contemporary society so willingly offers.

We therefore created an academic program that put a premium on inquiry-based learning, with an emphasis on projects and the continuous encouragement to ask intelligent questions. In the early days, students also took mini-courses in practical reasoning, ethics, and philosophy. The culmination of the academic program is the grade nine Masterworks requirement, wherein students work for six months with adult mentors to explore a project of personal interest (more on that later). The students also go on three expeditions a year—a hiking trip, a week long Discovery Week Trip, and a final kayak trip—and take monthly excursions to Vancouver to go skating or climbing or visit universities, art galleries, and museums. The school's extracurricular sport of choice is Ultimate Frisbee, which the students play with wild abandon in the fall and spring. During the winter, when they are not playing Ultimate, many of them rehearse for the Mainstage theatre event. There is also a cross-grade House system in which grade nine students take a leadership role. The House crews also take turns cleaning the school.

My naivety and financial acumen were also tested early on. In the year before the school started, I knew that I needed to raise about $50,000 in seed capital to get the thing up and operational. I happened to run into a local "professional fundraiser" who assured me that he had the contacts and know-how to raise the required funds. I accordingly paid him $10,000 in consulting fees from my own pocket, and he obligingly took all the money and raised not a dime. It was a humbling but ultimately valuable lesson to learn early in the process, because from that time on I became determined to keep a very sharp eye on every detail of the school's financial operation.

In 1995, our first year of operation, school fees were $3,750. The school has never received full revenue from student fees, however, because we introduced (and maintained) a fairly generous bursary program right from the beginning. Even though the school broke even or better every year, its funding history has been an interesting roller-coaster. I like to describe it as passing through three stages: the Peace Corps phase, where our fierce commitment to the project overlooked the fact that we paid ourselves a pittance; the Angel Donation phase, where benevolent donors propped up an untenable business plan because they loved what we were doing; and finally, the Sustainability Phase, where we had to start charging fees that would enable the school to have a future. School fees are now just over $16,000, with about 15% of the families receiving some level of financial assistance.

Enrollment gradually grew from 14 to 30 in the first four years, then hovered around 50 after we added a grade 6 class in 1999. After a few ups and downs, enrollment started to climb above 50 students in 2011 and reached its (now sustainable) level of 65 students in 2014. One of the most remarkable things that has happened in the last half decade is that families from the "continent" (i.e., the North Shore and Vancouver) have been choosing to send their children—by ferry, twice a day—to this little middle school on Bowen Island. The "off-island" contingent now makes up almost 50% of the school population.

There are many stories of IPS graduates who point to the school as being a significant pivot point in their lives—a time that challenged them and, in doing so, awakened them to the possibilities of who they might become. One student who was tenacious in her arguments in the Practical Reasoning course went on to study law at Oxford. Another, who flew a Cessna airplane on a grade eight excursion, earned her wings in the Canadian Air Force. A fourteen-year-old boy who completed a Masterworks on the theory of anarchy became a professor of political science. Another student, who thrived on the outdoor-pursuits trips, devoted herself to environmental service projects and then went on to start an organic farm.

My favourite story, though, is one about a painfully shy and unassuming young lady who eventually found the confidence to become a staff manager at a local retail outlet. This was the kind of kid who might have easily been ignored but instead quietly absorbed the encouragement and support of the school to go on and make something of herself. In different ways, all these students, and others, cite the hard work, commitment, and dedication of their IPS teachers as well as some of the special programs we created as the catalysts that made the difference.

Mainland families started sending their children to Island Pacific School because, after seventeen years of operation, it had earned a reputation for doing an exceptionally good job with middle school students. But it was a long and tough slog to get there. If I had known how difficult it was going to be to create and sustain this school, based on any prudent analysis I would not have done it. And yet, if I had done that analysis, the school would not exist today, the students would not have had the experiences they did, and I would not have had the opportunity to learn so many important things about education.

So, what did I learn? Three essential lessons that are, I believe, applicable for any school:

- We need to start with "why" before "how."

- We need to match our programs to our purposes.
- We need to teach our children well.

In the next three chapters, I will briefly explain what I mean by these lessons.

Island Pacific School: Lessons Learned

Lesson #1: Why Before How

In 1994, I had to walk into multiple living rooms in my local community and convince parents to send their children to a completely new school that I wanted to open the following year. This was, to put it mildly, a daunting proposition. It meant doing something that very few public school principals or heads of established independent schools ever have to do: offer an entire educational philosophy—from the ground up—that was compelling enough to convince people to risk their money and their children's future on an unproven experiment.

As difficult as this was, it turned out to be exactly the way I needed to begin. I have been struck, time and again, by how little contemporary conversation there is about the fundamental purposes of education and how quickly most of us accept the taken-for-granted default of our current system. Too much of the debate in contemporary schooling centers on the techniques of learning and instruction, with hardly anyone seriously asking what purposes these techniques are meant to serve.

This is fatal. For without clarity of purpose, we either run madly off in all directions or default, unthinkingly, to the status quo. In starting Island Pacific School, it became obvious that I first needed to make crystal clear—to parents, staff, and the students themselves—the "why before how" of the school, and indeed the value of a particular kind of education as a whole.

So how did I arrive at the "why before how" of Island Pacific School? I began by reflecting on the history of education and the tension between two fundamentally different views of its core purpose. According to one school of thought, education is understood as conveying the core intellectual and cultural traditions of a society. A good example would be the Great Books program[1] established by Mortimer Adler and Robert Maynard Hutchins, which sought to introduce students and adult learners to the seminal works and ideas of the Western tradition. Other examples include E.D. Hirsch's admonition that students acquire the "cultural literacy" they need to function in contemporary society[2] and William Bennett's prescriptions regarding the importance of an established core curriculum.[3]

There is also an entirely different tradition, which proposes that education should essentially concern itself with individual self-discovery. The historical antecedent is Jean Jacques Rousseau who proposed in his book, *Emile*, that the most appropriate way to cultivate a person's natural affinity for all things true and beautiful is to allow them to explore their own interests and desires. A.S. Neill's famous Summerhill School (in which students were not obligated to learn anything they did not want to) was a variation on this theme.[4] Whole generations of educators who have interpreted John Dewey as advocating "student-centered learning" are likewise descendants of this school of thought.

The caricatures and critiques of these different perspectives are vehement and relentless and have done much to undermine the value and contribution of each point of view.

Those who would see education as a matter of conveying intellectual and cultural traditions have been ridiculed as privileging the dominant viewpoints of a narrow band of "dead white males" (e.g., Aristotle and Shakespeare) to the exclusion of a purportedly broader and more humane rendering of the human story. Some critics of the intellectual and cultural traditions school argue, in fact, that there are no central intellectual and cultural traditions, i.e., that there are, and can only ever be, multiple traditions with no common ground. Taken to its logical extreme, this criticism negates the possibility of anything like a Universal Declaration of Human Rights or even a set of minimum responsibilities that we might expect people to adopt within what used to be called the "public sphere."

Critics of the self-discovery school, on the other hand, are wary of individual self-interest becoming the sole driver of the educative project. They are concerned that, at the very least, individual interest and choice will offer up a very shallow menu of educational possibilities, and at worst, it will be hopelessly self-indulgent. They sometimes fail to appreciate the extent to which human beings are, to a large extent, motivated by their interests and desires, and further, the notion that these interests need not always be narrow and base.

When we started Island Pacific School back in 1995, I looked for a way to combine the best of both traditions. I was much taken by University of Chicago president Robert Maynard Hutchins' insistence on initiating students into the "great conversations" of human inquiry. I liked the image of teachers bringing students to the edge of metaphorical tables where the seminal thinkers and creators of science, art, literature, mathematics, philosophy, and history were seated. I imagined that part of our job as teachers is to help students eavesdrop on their conversations.

But I also knew that, at the end of the day, the real gift of education was to help bring students to an understanding of their own capacities and interests. Although that understanding is derived, in part, from broad exposure to a series of experiences such as great conversations, we must also give students the tools and experiences they need to define for themselves how they are going to understand and make their way in the world.

I eventually found a way to blend and encapsulate these two traditions into a short form I could make intelligible. I told parents in those living rooms that our job as educators was to "initiate students into the great conversations of human inquiry, so they can find their own voice." While we later went on to create a broader and better description of the educative project, which I will describe in a later section of the book, the point is that it was crucial to start with—and continually discuss—a shared sense of purpose.

SHARING PURPOSE WITH PARENTS

I found that it was important to restate and reinforce our "why before how" formulation with parents at every opportunity I could find. I made sure that I made reference to it at the school year launch and found creative ways to carry on the conversation throughout the year. Sometimes we held "Education Roundtable" discussions with parents where we discussed broad educational issues. Once or twice a year, we might also do public presentations (for prospective and incumbent parents alike) on the philosophy and programs of the school. At other times, we would hold check-in meetings with parents to identify and discuss any items of concern. All of these venues provided an opportunity for us to re-examine what we were doing and why.[5]

I learned how important all of this was after I forgot to bring it to the surface for a while. I had been running the school for a few years and started to shift much of my focus to administrative management on the assumption that most parents "already knew" what the school was all about. But one day, I had a parent come and tell me that she had "lost the thread" as to the real value of the kind of education we were offering. At the next public meeting, I therefore made a point of reintroducing and illustrating our core purposes.

Parents want the best for their kids and, for the most part, want to be active and supportive participants in their child's development. If parents and schools clash, it is usually because there is a misunderstanding or disconnect about what each party is trying to achieve. I have had plenty of meetings where a half-hour conversation of mutual clarification was all that was needed to solve a miscue. These exchanges have always been worth it because when schools and parents co-commit to a shared set of goals, the way is clear to overcome all kinds of difficulties and create educational experiences of lasting value.

SHARING PURPOSE WITH TEACHERS

At Island Pacific School, I learned that the best way to have staff focus on issues of purpose is to *invite teachers to become educators*. In other words, we need to create opportunities for teachers to explore and appreciate "the big picture" challenges and potential of education. Moreover, they need to do this in a way that allows them to voice their aspirations for their students as well as their hopes and expectations about what they might contribute to the overall project.

Because teachers can so quickly get swept up in the day-to-day survival of lesson preparation, class management, student assessment, supervision duties, and extra-curricular events, they understandably sometimes lose the forest for the trees. But, if you want to create a better forest, this kind of reflection is essential.

Over the years, we approached this in different ways. During a pre-planning workshop in 2002, for example, the teachers and I mapped out the "tools" we wanted our students to acquire (e.g., basic literacies and emancipatory competencies) and then identified the "ways of being" we were hoping to instill. Between us we came up with the following list:

- A love of learning and a sense of intellectual curiosity
- A set of intellectual commitments and understandings
- A commitment to honesty
- A willingness to listen and be open-minded
- A willingness to persevere through difficult intellectual terrain
- A commitment to change one's mind on the basis of better reasons
- A commitment *not* to change one's mind unless given good reasons
- A set of moral commitments and understanding

- Respect for others
- Care and compassion for others
- A sense of responsibility for oneself
- A sense of confidence and hope

That year, we also had an interesting conversation about which elements of a complete education were properly contained within the jurisdiction of a school and which were not. We ended up assigning the school partial values to each component, knowing that external sources—parents, coaches, and community members—would complement our work.

Another year, we used the metaphor of a fire beneath a boiling cauldron to better understand our project. The cauldron was the form of our program. For example, the class sizes, the schedule, or the very structure of our school. The liquid in the cauldron was the curriculum, which included both academic subjects and extra-curricular opportunities for challenge and responsibility. The active boiling within the cauldron was the interaction of our students with the content of our school.

What was most important in this particular session were the sticks on the fire beneath the cauldron. For these were the teachers, or more precisely, the qualities and the commitments that they brought to the project. The idea was that each individual stick makes a unique contribution to the combined inferno that activates the entire operation. The question we were then required to ask ourselves was, "What sticks do we bring to the fire?"

To invite teachers to be educators is to engage them in basic questions of purpose: What are we trying to accomplish here and why? What do you think the point of this school's program is in the context of an overall education? How does the work you do contribute to this larger picture? While the uninitiated are sometimes puzzled—and even a little uncomfortable—in being confronted with these queries, over time they become increasingly animated.

Inviting teachers to be educators also means inviting them to become guardians of all that is worthwhile in education—to speak up when stupidity arises, yet at the same time be willing to do the hard work to create better solutions.

And finally, inviting teachers to become educators means inviting them to commit to the job not simply as a profession but as a calling.

If the educative project really is about "initiating students into great conversations so they can find their own voice"—or some such approximation—then this requires more from teachers than technical expertise in lesson planning and assessment. It requires their very hearts and souls.

SHARING PURPOSE WITH STUDENTS

Most schools have school mottos or, sometimes, a collection of virtues that are meant to represent the core values of the school. Our motto at Island Pacific School was "Learning. To Make a Difference." This proved to be so obvious and generic that it did not get discussed much, and therefore did not really seep into the consciousness of the students or the community at large. Our focus on the school's three targeted virtues—wisdom, courage, and integrity—was a different story, however.

When adults try to speak to students—particularly middle school students—about things like virtues, there is usually an overwhelming inclination for eyes to glaze over and minds to wander to other possible universes. Our challenge was to find a way to translate these three virtues into language they could understand.

We eventually described these core values in terms of our own aspirations for them as teachers, which at least had the virtue of being honest. We told them that when they graduated from grade nine, we wanted people to look at them and think, "There goes a kid with a head on his/her shoulders." We explained that this meant that people would regard them as knowledgeable and curious about the world. This was our middle school approximation of "wisdom."

Second, we said that people would see in them a warranted sense of confidence as a result of having met significant challenges—outdoor trips, Masterworks, etc. We were careful to make the distinction between confidence and arrogance, and explained that we wanted to see the former, not the latter. This was our middle school rendering of "courage."

Finally, we explained that we wanted people to look at them and conclude that they were decent human beings. In middle school shorthand, we said this meant that they should not throw rocks at people or otherwise be a jerk. We also told them that if they made a promise to someone and then something better came along, they needed to stick to their original promise. All of this was, in other words, our introductory approximation of "integrity."

Because we framed all of this in terms of our own aspirations, the call to live up to these virtues was an invitation they could choose to accept or not. When Frank Wiens at St. John's School spoke to a bunch of adolescent boys during chapel on Sunday night, he was doing the same thing: offering us a conception of the good that we could accept or reject. I think that sometimes we worry so much about unduly influencing the minds of the young that we end up giving them nothing at all. Or, more to the point, we end up leaving them with an unstated default that does not reflect conscious choice. We have a responsibility, certainly, to ensure that the virtues we offer students are morally defensible and worthwhile. But the point is that we need to make the invitation. And we need to simultaneously encourage and respect the emerging intelligence of young people to figure these things out for themselves.

At Island Pacific School, I learned that if you begin with "why before how" and are intentional about inviting parents, staff, and students to embrace the commitments therein, you can try all manner of programs and weather all sorts of storms in the pursuit of your collective goal. It is a principle that we need to apply when considering the future of grade school education at large. It is also a valuable principle for parents to keep in mind when assessing schools and in their conversations with principals, administrators, and teachers.

Island Pacific School: Lessons Learned

Lesson #2: Matching Program to Purpose

It is one thing to set more lofty goals for students; it is quite another to create a learning environment that gives them a real opportunity to achieve those goals.

At Island Pacific we faced a very practical challenge: how exactly do we "initiate students into great conversations so they can find their own voice?" How do we create an environment that encourages students to cultivate their capacity for "wisdom, courage and integrity?"

We employed different tactics on different fronts to deliver on these ambitious objectives. For example, I encouraged my teachers to locate their subject matter within a historical context by describing the personal achievements of various mathematicians, authors, musicians, scientists, artists, and philosophers and cross-referencing these with other developments at the time. We had our students go on outdoor expeditions to help them build confidence in their ability to overcome significant challenges (e.g., hiking to the top of the pass or spending a night in the woods). We had students clean the school as a compulsory obligation to help instill some measure of personal responsibility.

While we were not always successful in meeting our goals, the point is that we needed to try. We needed to match our program to our purpose. In what follows, I will sketch out two examples of programs at the school that were, I think, particularly successful in this regard.

PRACTICAL REASONING

I think it is fair to say that we are now enduring a growing cohort of citizens who fundamentally misunderstand or confuse some of the most basic intellectual and moral achievements that have been hard won over the past several centuries.

Take, for example, our current confusions about the status of "opinion" in our day-to-day conversations. For some reason, a good percentage of our population seems to believe that simply because a person has an opinion, this opinion should be afforded a kind of respect and taken seriously. Nothing could be further from the truth. The principle that "everyone has a right to their own opinion" does not mean that "every opinion is equally valid." People can be just plain wrong in the views they express.

This misunderstanding about the status of opinion is closely linked to a second confusion about the distinction between opinion and fact. As senator Daniel Patrick Moynihan so aptly put it, "You are entitled to your own opinion, but you are not entitled to your own facts."

Recently, we have seen alarming instances of the dangers that arise when a significant number of people begin to claim that all facts are "just" opinions. The facts of climate change, for example, are not something that one can have "opinions" about in the sense that they choose to believe them or not. They are facts.

The many irresponsible charges of "fake news" are another example. To claim that we live in a world of "fake news" is to issue a blanket denunciation of those in the media to the effect that none of what these people have to say can be trusted. This is a very basic fallacy (error in reasoning) known as an *ad hominem*. The mistake is to go against the person instead of addressing their argument itself.

These are very rudimentary mistakes and confusions that can, and should, be addressed in grade school. It is for this reason that I decided to introduce a weekly seminar in "Practical Reasoning"[1] for our grade six and seven students at Island Pacific School.

Practical reasoning is reasoning about human action——in other words, what one ought to do. Although it encompasses a vast domain in philosophy, the course offered to our middle school students at IPS was simply an introduction to some of the fundamentals of argument. This was not a course that offered up a grand set of generic "critical thinking skills," for as I will argue in the next section, we have good reason to be suspicious of these. It was, instead, a weekly workshop that introduced students to 1) a few basics like the distinction between types of claims, 2) some informal fallacies, and 3) the structure of deductive arguments. Let me expand a bit on each area to help convey the level and nature of enquiry we were encouraging with our middle school students.

Very briefly, empirical claims are claims of fact (for example, water boils at 100 degrees Celsius), and they are sustained by direct observation and/or experiment. Science is founded on empirical claims.

Conceptual claims are claims about the ordinary meaning or use of a word, and they are sustained by reference to ordinary language usage. A non-controversial conceptual claim is "All bachelors are unmarried men." A more controversial variant would be "A human embryo is a human being." In this case, what is at stake is what we mean by a human being (which then allows us to consider what human right we would attach to an embryo). Although conceptual claims can be employed anywhere, they most typically make their appearance in discourse about human affairs (e.g., philosophy, politics, and law).

Evaluative claims are claims of value, and they can be rendered as standards (for example, "that is a good pen"; "that was a horrible movie") or principles (you should not throw rocks at people). Evaluative claims are sustained, in the case of standards, by reference to agreed upon evaluative criteria (e.g., what makes a pen a good pen?) and, in the case of principles, by reference to a variety of higher-order tests that human beings, as the result of contemplation and experience over many centuries, have come to find compelling. Some examples: How would you like it if someone threw rocks at you? What would it look like if everyone threw rocks at each other? What is the likelihood that the pain and fear a victim will experience far surpasses any short-lived delight you might feel in throwing the rock? How does throwing rocks at a victim uphold or offend a more fundamental principle such as, for example, respect for persons?

With a bit of work on our part, these distinctions eventually became understandable to the middle school students at our school. While they may not have remembered all the fine points, our basic goal was that they be able to recognize that the proposition "Water boils at 100 degree Celsius" is a different kind of claim than "Bachelors are unmarried men," or "This is a good pen," and that each requires a different kind of defense.

This matters because, in common discourse, people mix these up all the time and then talk at cross purposes. See if you can notice this in your next "argumentative" conversation.

Informal fallacies are intentional or unintentional mistakes in reasoning. As we saw, the *ad hominem* fallacy makes the mistake of attacking the person rather than the argument they are presenting (e.g., a politician degrading another politician without directly addressing the issue at hand). The hasty generalization fallacy makes the mistake of drawing a conclusion from a limited sample size (e.g., Last week, a teenager stole something from a store. Teenagers these days are nothing but a bunch of thieves). The appeal to popularity fallacy makes the mistake of concluding that, if many people believe or like something, it must be true or worthy of endorsement (e.g., Millions of people believe in astrology. There must be some truth to it).

These fallacies, and many others like them, are committed all the time. Again, check it out. By introducing our students to such fallacies in the middle school years, we hoped to heighten their awareness of the many diversions to clear thinking they would encounter not only for the rest of their education, but also for the rest of their lives.

The main purpose in introducing students to the structure of deductive arguments was to get them to see the difference between a premise and a conclusion and the fact that the former is meant to support the latter. For example, the two claims that "Other things being equal, we should not cause harm to others" (an evaluative claim) and "Your actions, in fact, caused harm to your classmate" (an empirical claim) are premises that can be used informally to support the conclusion that "You should not have acted in that way to your classmate."[2]

Having students gain a feel for how premises connect (and do not connect) to conclusions eventually enables them to spot *non sequiturs*, i.e., cases where a proposed conclusion does not follow from the premises. One example might be "He is regarded as a successful businessman; therefore, he should become Prime Minister."

The concepts and distinctions that we introduced in the practical reasoning workshops were the most basic introductory building blocks to a more complete understanding of human action. They were meant to complement and illuminate the contextual knowledge that students were being exposed to in their regular subject area classes. They were tools that students could use to better evaluate the multitudinous claims in the world around them. But the workshops also offered a fundamental proposition: that we should *care* that people have their facts right and *care* that they can provide a coherent defence for evaluative propositions.

Isaac Asimov once said that the anti-intellectualism that permeates our political and cultural life is "nurtured by the false notion that democracy means that 'my ignorance is just as good as your knowledge'."[3] If we do not give students the tools to build a democracy that is founded on something better than ignorance, we as a community and a society will get what we deserve.

MASTERWORKS

The Masterworks program at Island Pacific School was explicitly designed to encourage students to discover and develop their own interests, capabilities, or passions. Although we had provided some opportunities for students to do this in their regular program by way of personal interest-driven variations on projects or assignments in class, the Masterworks program was a stand-alone capstone project for our graduating grade nine students that would call upon all their intellectual and creative resources.

Here is how it works. In early October, the students select a topic of personal interest. For the next seven months, they work with an advisory committee to develop their ideas and/or create whatever it is they chose to create. Along the way, they produce a 15- to 25-page paper. At the end of the school year, they stand up and publicly defend their work to an audience of 100-150 people.

It is important that students select a topic that interests them as opposed to something that interests their parents or teachers. As an aside, it is remarkable how rarely young people are asked what they think about things or what their interests are. When I interviewed students who were interested in coming to Island Pacific School, I occasionally described the Masterworks program and asked what question they might pursue if given this opportunity. Some of these ten-year-old students immediately shared their great curiosity about spiders or dinosaurs or what people wore in the Middle Ages. Others, however, were completely baffled by the question. Sadly, they did not have much experience following through on their own questions, particularly when asked in the context of a school. This made it all the more important that, in the Masterworks program, the question or idea came from the student.

The topics and projects students select have been incredibly diverse. Here are just a few examples:[4]

- The Many Worlds Interpretation in Quantum Mechanics
- Between the Lines (A Film Short)
- An Overview of Developed World Automobile Emissions
- Remixing the Moonwalk: Teaching the School to Dance Like the King of Pop
- Fractals and Chaos: Exploring Reality
- Chad Is Making a Guitar!
- The Pressure to Be Perfect: Western Society's Approach to Body Image
- Is Euthanasia Morally Defensible?

One of the keys to making the program work is the structure of support. Each student has an advisory committee consisting of a teacher as the internal Chair and one or two External Faculty who are adult volunteers outside the school with an interest in the topic being investigated. The job of the chair is to host the meetings and keep the writing and discovery process moving along. The External Faculty, who are often experts in the field, attend four to five advisory meetings and assist the student with advice and resources. There is something very compelling about having a 14-year-old student sit with three adults to discuss an area of shared interest.

The 15- to 25-page paper differs in content and format depending on the subject. Often, these are expository reviews of the question under investigation. In cases where students create something—a handmade guitar, a one-person play, a refurbished motorcycle, a novella—the paper usually takes the form of journal reflections about the process. At some point in their written work, the student is obliged to address the question "Why should we care?" as a way to link their personal exploration to larger questions.

The actual Masterworks presentations take place in June. Students have 20 minutes to present, after which they take questions from their advisory committee and then questions from the floor. The entire school attends, along with parents and members of the community. It is important that the younger students also be allowed to ask questions as part of their own introduction into public discourse.

The Masterworks projects are not "marked" in any typical fashion. Directly after the full presentation, the student's advisory committee meets briefly with the student to give immediate feedback on how things went. This usually takes the form of a brief "sandwich" discussion that first touches on what went well, then moves on to one or two things that might be considered for "next time," and finishes with a hearty congratulations on having completed such a formidable task. In a sense the Masterworks projects are therefore assessed on a pass/fail basis, where "pass" means completion and "fail" means that the project was not completed. In 24 years of presenting Masterworks projects at Island Pacific School, no student has ever failed. While it is true—particularly in the early years—that some presentations danced on the edges of intelligibility, the quality of student work has consistently improved over the years as a direct result of the quality of support we learned to provide. The real "assessment and evaluation" within this project is the ongoing feedback from committee members and the questions and responses in the public presentation.

While the Masterworks program clearly and intentionally is driven by student interest, it is also explicitly designed as a catalyst to introduce bigger connective ideas. I once worked with a student who wanted to do something on "Comedy" for his Masterworks. This student was a clever young man who was also a bit of a jokester and essentially just wanted to do a brief stand-up routine as his presentation. For the paper part of the project, we asked him to first survey different types of comedy by watching and taking notes on different types of comedians and explaining the different techniques and elements that go into the construction of a stand-up routine. In our committee meetings, we pushed him on some of the bigger questions of comedy such as "What makes something funny?" and "To what extent, if any, does comedy define us as human beings?" What we were really hoping for, of course, was that a 14-year-old middle school kid who simply wanted to do a comedy routine would eventually come to see just how complex and rich comedy really is, and how fundamentally representative it is of who we are as human beings. Only time will tell if we were successful in that regard.

While these two programs—Practical Reasoning and Masterworks—likely had a significant effect on IPS students, neither of them was part of the standard Ministry of Education curriculum. They were, however, operational expressions of some of the school's core purposes: to move students more closely toward some approximation of "wisdom" and create authentic opportunities for them to discover and develop their personal interests and abilities.

For me, the lesson was that sometimes we need to strike out on our own to create the most valuable learning experiences for our students.

Island Pacific School: Lessons Learned

Lesson #3: Teach Your Children Well

When we first started Island Pacific School, I regarded "development of character" as something of an add-on to the school's central academic purpose. My first priority back then was to give students an academic education worthy of the name. The emphasis on inquiry-based learning, the introduction of practical reasoning, and the Masterworks program were all designed with this in mind.

What I also came to realize, however, was that in addition to needing to be intellectually challenged, adolescents also desperately need—and, in fact, want—a compelling and defensible picture of how they ought to "be." They are often preoccupied with assessing various models of behaviour and analyzing or judging what is the right thing to do in different life situations—and they are ready to explore any narrative that might be worthy of their attention.

Many schools fail to address this fundamental adolescent need for deeper engagement around questions of behaviour. A school may pride itself on maintaining safe, orderly learning environments, ensuring that its students do not impinge on the rights of others and preserving a sense of fairness in its disciplinary dealings. But in most cases, the overall goal is simply preserving school order rather than advancing the deeper—and more challenging—educative mission of building character and fostering an authentic sense of responsibility among students. As a result, schools rarely seem to take full advantage of the profound and timely opportunities for learning that can emerge simply by establishing expectations around student behaviour.

So, what was our approach at IPS? We learned quickly that it was one thing to talk to middle school students about having "heads on their shoulders" and quite another to create an environment that enabled such aspirations to eventually take hold. After all, we were faced with the full range of predictable adolescent challenges and distractions that stood in the way of allowing kids to discover and express their very best selves. It turned out that the key was establishing a fairly specific set of baseline behavioural expectations as the fertile soil that would eventually encourage and allow more substantive virtues to emerge.

This was, in other words, all about the creation of *school culture*, which essentially had to do with establishing the tone of the place. We found that the mechanics of creating a school culture involved being very intentional about "norm setting," i.e., continuously laying out, in clear language, the expectations and aims of the community. This happened on two levels. First there were the obvious *behavioural* expectations that need to be in place in order to have a clean, safe, and respectful learning environment (pick up your garbage, don't be a bully, be polite). Then there were the *aspirational* expectations such as try your best, be a decent human being, don't follow the crowd, have good reasons for things, broaden your mind, cultivate your curiosity, put care and diligence into everything you do, and don't be afraid of failure.

Norm setting requires both front end and back end interventions. On the front end, it is a matter of making clear the behavioural expectations and at the same time being intentional and specific about communicating the aspirational goals of the community.

One simple example from IPS was our requirement that students stand up at the beginning of each class when their teacher entered the room. We took time, at the beginning of each year, to explain to the students what this was about. We told them that it was not really about being polite to the teacher (although we said it is always good to be polite), nor was it about showing special deference to the teacher. Rather, it was about re-confirming a reciprocal relationship of trust and respect and, at the same time, mutually identifying the core project at hand. You see, the second (and equally important) part of this little protocol was that, upon entering the class and seeing the students standing, the *teacher* looked each student in the eyes and said, "Thank you for being here" to the entire class. We explained that the trust and respect was meant to cut both ways—that teachers should respect and acknowledge the students just as much as the students should respect and acknowledge the teachers. We also explained the most important thing: teachers and students alike are on a kind of "sacred ground" in classrooms where learning and the cultivation of their best selves is meant to occur. Thus, these small gestures were meant to strike deep to the core of the school's entire ethos.

There were two dimensions to the "backend interventions" we employed at IPS. On one hand, we had predictable consequences that were delivered by way of a fairly formal discipline interventions progression. More importantly, though, we used the inevitable transgressions of middle school students as an opportunity to introduce a larger life lesson.

The discipline interventions progression we used is likely similar to many that exist in other schools, although we began with very minor infractions before building up to more serious matters. Level One, for example, occurred when a student interrupted someone else in class. When that happened, they had to immediately stand up, look the person in the eye, apologize, and then sit down. The whole thing was over in about ten seconds, and the class moved on. Level Two happened, for example, when a student persistently interrupted or distracted a class. The student was taken out of the class where the teacher looked him or her in the eye, underlined what the problem was, and made clear the new expectation. This took about a minute and, again, the class moved on. The student knew, however, that this was a "Level Two" encounter.

Level Three was reserved for slightly more egregious behaviour such as persistent disruptions or poor treatment of another student. The consequence was that it would be dealt with by the Head or Assistant Head of School, with parents usually brought into the loop. Although the consequences could take many forms, they more often than not involved one or two lunches in the Head's Office.

At Level Four, the student had done something significantly problematic, usually involving intentional harm to others or the community (such as bullying or stealing). The consequence here was a suspension, either in-school or out-of-school. The message we wanted to send to the student and the parent was that the student had done something to offend the community in a significant way, and that if they were not prepared to change their behaviour, they would not be able to stay.

Level Five was expulsion. This happened when it was abundantly clear that the student had no interest in or capacity to contribute in a positive way to the school community.

We learned three important things about the use of this progression. The first was that we needed to make this discipline progression very transparent to parents at the beginning of the year before any little "adventures" unfolded. It was important to explain how the progression worked, the inevitability of their children experiencing consequences within this progression, and the value of them doing so.

The second thing we learned was how beneficial this progression was for the staff, particularly for those teachers who had problems with basic classroom management. The stand up/thank you protocol coupled with the Level

One interruption intervention went a long way toward setting the necessary ground rules regarding community interactions and mutual respect.

The third and most important thing we learned, however, was that by making this entire progression of consequences completely clear to the students in advance, and by immediately and consistently intervening with students at Levels One and Two, *we rarely got to Levels Three and Four and almost never got to Level Five.* We found, in other words, that by establishing clear expectations about so-called "little things"—interrupting in class, using inappropriate language—we created an environment where we very rarely had to deal with more serious matters.

This progression of "consequences" was only one operational component of a much larger life lesson we wanted to teach our students. At Island Pacific School, we told the kids up front that they were going to do things at the school and in their lives that they would not be proud of. We explained that adults do these things as well. We then further explained that what matters most is *how they conduct themselves* when transgressions occur. And then we gave them the template that we were going to use at the school to show them how to behave and what ought to happen when things went wrong.

It went like this. First, we again emphasized that we will, in fact, do things we are not proud of. Sometimes we will act impulsively without thinking things through. Sometimes we will accept invitations from peers to do stupid things. Both of these are particularly prevalent amongst middle school students, by the way. And sometimes, we know we should not do something, but we create some sort of rationalization why it might be okay after all. (Adults especially like to pull this one.)

We then explained to the students that the first and most difficult thing they need to do when things go wrong is take full responsibility for their actions—to admit that they did, in fact, throw the rock through the window or call that person a nasty name or whatever it was.

This truly was the most difficult thing because, when we are called out on our behaviour, our immediate instinct is to try and dodge the bullet, to flat-out deny the allegation or point the finger elsewhere. It takes a certain amount of internal fortitude to admit that you have done something wrong. This is particularly hard for young people because, despite appearances, they want to be regarded well by the adults around them. It is, however, the kind of thing that needs to be confronted early in life, because if it is not, you can end up with an adult who is pathologically immature. We have all seen these people: individuals who are incapable of taking responsibility for their own actions, who habitually point to "the other guy" as the source of the problem when things go wrong, or who invariably create wild rationalizations or outright lies to cover their tracks. It is especially important, therefore, that we emphasize to young people the importance of "owning their own behaviour" as the first step in a moral and operational template to use when they do something wrong.

The second thing that needed to happen was, of course, consequences.

What is great about middle school is that we get to arrange "proxy" consequences for relatively innocuous transgressions that nonetheless serve as impactful "teachable moments." We once had some students who left garbage lying around on the ferry. The very next day, they were back on the ferry working with the crew washing tables and vacuuming. We also had a kid who made a particular mess in the school and did not, at first, own up to it. When he eventually admitted responsibility, he spent half a Saturday washing desks. Although these consequences were real enough to the students who experienced them, they were still proxies for the more serious consequences that would inevitably follow, should a person fail to take responsibility for themselves in the future.

The third element within the "When Things Go Wrong" template was the requirement to, in some fashion, make amends. When we had students apologize to their colleagues, or vacuum the ferry, or clean desks on a Saturday, the hope was that they see the importance of attempting to make restitution when they had done something wrong. Sometimes, this could come across as artificial as it was. For example, I once had two students in my office who were obligated to apologize to one another. That said, I think it is important to give students—middle school students in particular—a model of what it looks like to handle difficult situations with integrity. Aristotle once said that "One enters the house of virtue through the portal of habit." Having kids habitually make amends when things go wrong provides opportunities for these habits to take root.

The fourth piece in teaching students to work through difficult situations is to encourage them to *learn* from their mistakes. The idea is to have them take a few moments to review how things went wrong and see if they can figure out how not to go down that road again. This should most definitely *not* take the form of a long sermon, but should rather just be a quick "Hey, think about this" kind of invitation. Kids are not stupid; they already know what went wrong. For some people, all it takes is one time. If one is dealing with impulsive middle school students, however, there will likely be frequent opportunities to re-introduce this particular "teachable moment."

The final step in the template is to *move on*. When we do something that we are not proud of, the most important things to do are to take responsibility for our actions, deal forthrightly with the consequences, make amends, and try to learn from the experience. If all those things are done with integrity, you have done all that you can do, and you should move on. There is no point in either the teacher or the student continuing to dwell on the negative behaviour. Instead, the idea is to put things back into perspective and create a fresh chapter.

Did the students at Island Pacific School always adopt and embrace the behavioural and aspirational expectations of the school? Of course not. But most of the time, most of them did. More importantly, they left the school having been exposed to at least one reasonably coherent narrative about how they might behave in the world and what they might aspire to.

Needless to say, it was critical for parents to be more or less aligned with our intentions. Sometimes, however, the parents were not particularly good allies. I remember an incident involving three girls who were being rambunctious while waiting in a passenger shelter for their commuter ferry. For some reason, they kicked a plexiglass window and broke it. I heard about this and contacted the three sets of parents to let them know that part of the resolution would be that the girls pay for the damages. I received three different responses to this proposition. The first was immediate acceptance of the plan and clear support for the idea that the girls need to take full responsibility for their actions. The second offered only begrudging support because the mom wanted to challenge how much *her* daughter was involved and what portion she ought to pay. The third parent flat-out refused to have her daughter pay. She said, remarkably, that "BC Ferries has insurance for that kind of thing," with the implication that it should not be up to girls to pay for the damages.

In another story, we had a family living off-island with a son at the school whose attendance was erratic. On one occasion, I asked the young man why he had been away, and he explained that he was sick and had to spend the day in bed. I subsequently learned that he was not sick at all, and had, in fact, played basketball during the evening in question. A few days later, I had a meeting with the parents and asked them about his absence. With completely straight faces they explained that he had been ill for several days. In other words, they flat-out lied. Is it any wonder that the boy himself did the same?

There are some who would say that the youth of today are immoral, lazy, irresponsible, and entitled. The truth is that *they are what we make them*. My experience is that most young people are more than willing to be good-natured, industrious, responsible, respectful, and honest if given the right support and direction. If kids end up being otherwise, it is because they have had people whom they ought to have trusted leading them down another path.

Thankfully, the majority of our parents were on our side. The kid who came into the school to wash desks on Saturday did so with the blessing of his parents. Our working assumption was that the school should simply complement what families were already doing at home along these lines, and this turned out to be the case most of the time.

A final story: Island Pacific School has a philosophy when it comes to language. Students are expected to refrain from using lazy and offensive language in their day-to-day interactions. They are not supposed to say, "Shut up" or "That sucks" and they are most certainly not supposed to swear. We explained that the language that people use is reflective of the quality of their thoughts and their capacity for self-discipline. We pointed out that it is easy to default to the common denominator of phrases like "shut up" and "that sucks" and, of course, swearing. We then invited, encouraged, and expected students to be intentional about taking their language up a notch as one way to express the very best of who they are.

Despite these eloquent admonitions, we had an instance where one of our students was out of school, walking through the community to the ferry, and swearing like the proverbial sailor. It happened that an elderly neighbour heard him and telephoned the school to let me know that she was not impressed. This was actually a good thing because it presented a golden opportunity to arrange a little "object lesson" in social civility for this young man. I asked the neighbour whether she would mind having the student over to receive his apology for his behaviour. After some hesitation and encouragement from me about helping a kid get headed in the right direction, she agreed. I talked to the student and explained to him why his behaviour was unacceptable, what his consequences would be, and how he was going to make amends for this transgression. I also asked the student's mom if we could proceed with this reconciliation, and she was very supportive.

On the designated day, we went over to the neighbour's house, and the student dutifully apologized. A couple of interesting things happened in the course of this exchange. First, the boy was able to see that he wasn't the centre of the universe, his actions had an effect on others, and he needed to take account of the legitimate interests of those around him. Second, the neighbour was able to see that most young people are actually decent human beings who sometimes just need a little nudge in the right direction. The final part of the equation is for the offended person to actually accept the other person's apology. This person did this in spades; we had some tea and cookies and a nice little chat. The student got to be acknowledged for having the integrity to apologize, and the woman got to see that kids are okay after all.

While not all of our interventions went this well, enough of them did to keep us going. While I was frankly annoyed at times about having to spend so much time and energy on these sorts of things, I eventually came to see them as central to the larger project of helping kids make their way in the world. In some cases, it takes many pebbles in a pond to help people find their best selves, and indeed some never do. The point is that we need to keep trying. Whether it be in schools, on soccer pitches, or at home, we can't ever abdicate our responsibility to pay attention to the emerging character of those in our charge.

Island Pacific School: Lessons Learned

Moving On

I was happy and proud to be associated with Island Pacific School at its founding and through its development over 22 years. I had a beautiful opportunity to learn many things there, and I am grateful for the important contributions we were able to make to the lives of many of our students. Nonetheless, I am acutely aware of its limitations as a model that might be adopted on a broader scale. It is an independent school that is financially out of reach for many families. It is a small school that has the unusual luxury of being able to create an intentional and collegial community where teachers and administrators have the opportunity to know their students well and have the freedom and flexibility to design programs to match its purposes. It is a middle school that has built educational experiences and a school environment for students, many elements of which would not be appropriate in an elementary or senior secondary setting. And its reach has been limited; over the past two decades, IPS has graduated about 250 grade nine students.

Perhaps more important than any of this, however, is the hard reality that, for all its advantages, IPS was still not able to serve every one of its students equally well. This is a problem, writ large, in the architecture of almost all contemporary schools. I call it the "great compromise" of grade school education.

Very imperfectly put, most current learning cohorts typically have three types of learners: fast, medium, and slow. For a variety of reasons, what usually happens in schools is that most teachers teach to the middle group. They create lessons and exercises aimed at the "mainstream" cohort and then, when they can, try to manage a few tweaks for the gifted and those who struggle. These tweaks, however, are rarely as effective as they need to be. The "lower" level students do not receive the concentrated support they need, while "higher" level students are not challenged enough. But it is also the case that the so-called mid-range students need more. These are the wallflower students who are competent and quiet enough not to draw the attention of teachers. They get by "well enough" within the system because they complete the assignments on time and do—more or less—what is asked of them. What they do not get is an education that challenges and inspires them to expand their capacity. The great compromise within contemporary schools, therefore, is that nobody gets what they really need.

At Island Pacific School, we were able to mitigate some of these difficulties by virtue of our small size and the commitment of our teachers and learning support staff to reach every student. We also looked for opportunities via extensions and special projects to challenge and engage our students. But, in spite of all of this, there were still "the ones that got away"—the students who left the school because we were unable to unlock the door that would enable them to flourish. This is one of the many things that kept me awake at night.

Ever since, this problem of "the ones that got away" has had me thinking that there must be something we can do beyond inserting mere tweaks into the system. If we want to create impactful schools for all students, we need to start thinking about a complete structural reorganization of what we are doing. We can't just mount a GPS on the dashboard of our clunker; we need to get a new car. Or, more precisely, we need to start thinking differently about "transportation" as a whole.

There is a second problem that has also troubled me. While I appreciated the luxury—and accepted the challenge—of building a new school from the ground up, I am very mindful, again, that independent and private schools serve only 6.8% of the student population in Canada and about 10% of students in the United States. The fact remains that over 90% of students in Canada and the USA receive their education through traditional public schools. If we are interested—as I am—in creating impactful education for all students, we will need to consider how the ideas presented in this book might somehow find their way into public schools.

For the remainder of the book, therefore, I am going to move beyond the particulars of Island Pacific School and explore how grade school education as a whole might be reshaped in a way that will allow students and educators to get the best out of one another. Before I do that, however, it will be useful to briefly consider where we have come from in grade school education and where we appear to be going.

You Are Here

From the Dominant Model to the Ascendant Model

FROM THE DOMINANT TO THE ASCENDANT MODEL

Our school systems are shaped and defined by an interconnected constellation of premises, assumptions, and implicit practices about which we may be unaware and indeed which we may find extremely problematic. For the past 40 years (at least), that constellation has been subtly shifting from what might be called the "Dominant" model to what I call the "Ascendant" model of educational delivery. While we are well rid of most elements of the Dominant model, and while there are certain elements of the Ascendant model that have real promise, we need to be careful that we do not replace the Dominant model with something that once again fails to live up to the true potential of education.

THE DOMINANT MODEL OF SCHOOLING

By Dominant model, I'm referring to the system of education that has dominated the North American landscape during most of the 20th century and that has elements that persist to this day. This view of schooling and education might also be called the "human capital" or "technical" or "factory school" model of education. Its core elements are as follows:

- Its explicit purpose was to train and socialize students to participate in the economic structure of society.
- It transformed the pursuit of knowledge into a process of fact accumulation at the expense of genuine understanding.
- It trained teachers to deliver a set curriculum.
- It had the effect (if not the explicit purpose) of favouring and accrediting students in reference to a narrow band-width of ability.

The schools that we have today were shaped, in large part, at the beginning of the 20th century as institutions explicitly designed to prepare people for "the world of work." You might be surprised to learn how explicit this intent was. Elwood Cubberly, the eventual Dean of Education at Stanford University, had this to say in his 1905 dissertation for Columbia Teachers' College:

Schools should be factories in which raw products, children, are to be shaped and formed into finished products...manufactured like nails, and the specifications for manufacturing will come from government and industry.[1]

This notion that schools should be places that "shape and form" children into "products" according to the specifications of "government and industry" championed a view of schooling that saw its ultimate rationale as one of ensuring that students would have the ability to fulfill and sustain the occupational requirements of the newly-evolving industrial economy.

This view aligned well with certain other assumptions that were becoming dominant at the time, most notably the idea that people could be efficiently "formed" to meet the required specifications of the "new economy" by way of proper organizational methods.

In his groundbreaking book, The End of Average, Todd Rose demonstrates how the "scientific management" principles of Frederick Taylor (which became known as Taylorism) came to dominate the operational structure of both factories and schools. In the quest to become more efficient in processing large numbers of students through a necessarily uniform curriculum, educational leaders created and embraced the fictional notion of the "average student" as the essential presupposition which then enabled them to standardize their instructional processes and organizational structure.

The initial idea seemed to be that by standardizing an education system around the presumed average capacities of students, we would become more efficient at creating the "average man" needed to fill the requirements of the emerging industrial economy. Rose writes, "The educational Taylorists declared that the new mission of education should be to prepare mass numbers of students to work in the newly Taylorized economy."[2]

These developments in schools copied and adopted the systems of mass production then being perfected in factories. Henry Ford's automobile plants—in which he used an assembly line format to produce a complete automobile every three minutes—became the standard of modern-day efficiency. It was an efficiency, however, dependent upon a uniformity of product. It was famously said of the Ford Model-T that "any customer can have a car painted any colour that he wants, so long as it is black.

Rose further explains how this standardization came to be transported into schools:

> Schools around the country adopted the "Gary Plan", named after the industrialized Indiana City where it originated: students were divided into groups by age (not by performance, interest, and aptitude) and these groups of students rotated through different classes, each lasting a standardized period of time. Schools bells were introduced to emulate factory bells, in order to mentally prepare children for their future careers.[3]

The second defining characteristic of the Dominant model of education has been its profound distortion of the role that knowledge plays in understanding. To put it most succinctly, the dominant model of schooling emphasized facts—and facts alone—in isolation from context. While there is nothing wrong with knowing some facts—for indeed these make up part of the necessary foundation to understanding—the problem comes when we "teach" facts in isolation from any overall context or explanatory framework.

One key reason for this may be that the identification and demonstrated acquisition of discrete facts (i.e., by way of correct answers on factual recall tests) is easier to both teach and measure than the more general attribute we call understanding. If a teacher does not really understand the defining characteristics of mathematics, art, literature, science, philosophy, or history, it is much easier to make designated definitions, dates, and formulas the essential curriculum of a course. Similarly, it is much easier to measure and report on the acquisition of facts than the somewhat more nebulous, but infinitely more important, achievement of understanding.

A third defining characteristic of the dominant model of education is that it regards teachers as technicians, i.e., as competent practitioners whose job is to effectively deliver the course. There is a whole educational literature on "effective schools" and "effective teaching" that conveys the idea that to be a "good" teacher, one simply accumulates a bag of instructional strategies—best practices, if you will—and then deploys these in the delivery of a curriculum. The implication is that if one effectively communicates the facts, learning will occur. From this view, teachers are little more than sophisticated assembly line workers who add components as a student moves through the system.

The fourth and perhaps most problematic feature of the Dominant model was the way it sorted and classified students on the basis of a very narrow range of abilities. Todd Rose explains that while the early educational Taylorists "argued that the goal of education was to provide every student with the same average education to prepare them for the same average jobs"[4], this orientation changed with the arrival on the scene of psychologist Edward Thorndike. Thorndike believed that "the purpose of schools was not to educate all students to the same level but to sort them according to their innate level of talent."[5]

...schools should [instead] sort young people according to their ability so they could efficiently be appointed to their proper station in life, whether manager or worker, eminent leader or disposable outcast—and so that educational resources could be allocated accordingly.[6]

Thorndike thought that there would be winners and losers in this educational selection game. The talented would proceed to colleges and then positions of leadership, the average would go straight from high school into more mundane jobs, and educational resources spent on slow-learning students should be reduced or eliminated.[7] "Success" within this environment was predicated on a rather narrow range of abilities and dispositions, i.e., a compliant disposition matched with an ability to remember facts and write neatly. This system was both cruel and incredibly wasteful in the way it marginalized and effectively discredited people who were otherwise perfectly capable, creative, and intelligent but nonetheless did not fit into the factory-school mold.

Even though the features above describe a North American school system as it was emerging about a century ago, most parents and educators will recognize residues of it within our current schools and those of the recent past. For example, we still group students according to age (rather than performance, interest, or aptitude); we still have standardized class times; we still define and sort students on the basis of their deviation from average (below average, above average, superior); and, remarkably enough, we still have bells in schools, even though most contemporary workplaces did away with these long ago.

THE ASCENDANT MODEL OF SCHOOLING

Based on a multitude of critiques from the 1960s onward,[8] many aspects of the Dominant model began to give way to what I call the Ascendant model. This is the system of education that emerged, in infant form, in the late

1960s and is now approaching critical mass during the beginning of the 21st century. Some of its most noteworthy characteristics are as follows:

- It embraces "student-centered learning" and "personalized learning" as its core operational practices.
- It de-emphasizes the acquisition of knowledge as a requisite to understanding and focuses instead on the development of generic "skills"—"thinking" skills; "collaboration" skills, etc.—as the key to 21st century learning.
- It emphasizes instructional technique divorced from purpose.

There is much within this Ascendant model that is positive and worthy of our endorsement. There is a growing awareness, for example, that different students learn differently, and a corresponding interest in finding better ways to meet their individual needs. This is all to the good.

There is also, however, a lot of jargon associated with contemporary education, and people frequently mean different things when using the same terms. Student-centered learning and personalized learning, for example, are partially overlapping concepts, with personalized learning being a distinctive subset of student-centered learning. In order to get a better sense of where we have arrived, it will be useful to sort through some of these concepts. A clear understanding of them might also be helpful in enabling parents and educators to better understand one another.[9]

STUDENT-CENTERED LEARNING

The easiest way to understand "student-centered learning" is to contrast it against some of its apparent opposites. Student-centered learning is sometimes meant to be different from "teacher-centered learning" in that, with student centered learning, the student—not the teacher—sets the learning agenda. There is, for example, a place in British Columbia called Choice School For the Gifted and Exceptional that presents itself as offering a flexible learning environment for "bright, creative, and engaged" students that allows them, in part, to follow their own interests because "their curiosity has taken them there."[10] There is another program called Self-Design Global that caters to the homeschool market and proposes explicitly that "children deserve to have an educational experience that speaks to them, engages dynamically with their interests, and fosters their own learning styles."[11] They invite homeschooling parents to create a "more fluid and learner-centered process than what is provided by the traditional school setting." This expression of student-centered learning is therefore meant to shift at least some of the responsibility for learning from the teacher to the student.

A second contrast presumably embedded with student-centered learning is the distinction between active and passive learning. Traditional (factory-school) education is sometimes described as "passive," wherein the student passively receives the knowledge of the teacher. Student-centered education, on the other hand, is presumed to be active, where the student actively engages in their own learning. In this version, students do so because they are interested in the subject matter or they find it more relevant.

The general idea in this version of a student-centered learning approach is that the student will have some say about what they will learn and, as a result, will be actively engaged in their own learning.

There is a separate but related variation of student-centered learning that is grounded in the psychological theories of Lev Vygotsky, Jean Piaget, and John Dewey. Very simply put, the core idea is that students must be given the opportunity to actively construct their own understanding of things if they are ever going to have the chance of authentic learning. For example, instead of a teacher simply telling students about, and having them memorize, the Pythagorean formula for discovering the length of the diagonal in a right triangle, the teacher must engineer a set of explorations that will allow students to discover for themselves how that formula works. In this version of student-centered learning (sometimes called discovery learning, inquiry-based, or authentic learning), the emphasis is on the quality of the learning. Teachers must use their understanding of cognitive development to create learning environments that enable students to eventually figure things out "for themselves."

Clearly, there are some powerful ideas here. Other things being equal, if we can enable students to have more ownership and engagement in their own learning, this is all to the good. This is precisely what the IPS Masterworks projects were all about, and it's something I think we need more of, particularly in the senior secondary years. That said, there are nonetheless a few reasons to be cautious about embracing all of this *en masse*.

If, by student-centered learning, we mean that most of the curriculum that students are exposed to should be driven by their own interests—what they perceive as relevant—there are a couple of obvious objections. The first is that we cannot know, in advance, if we will be interested in something until we are exposed to it. This relates to the second objection: that part of our responsibility as educators is to broaden the horizons of our students to give them a deeper and richer reservoir out of which to eventually define themselves. It is an easy thing for me, as a teacher, to "engage" my students by simply having them do things they enjoy. I likely do them more of a service, however, when I introduce new and unfamiliar ideas as part of a larger project to enable them to make better sense of the world and themselves within it. The introductions to practical reasoning and the initiations into great conversations at IPS were presented to the students at IPS with this in mind.

With regard to that variant of student-centered learning that would have teachers carefully engineer their learning environments to bring about authentic learning, two observations are worthy of note. The first is a reminder that it is very much the teachers who are choosing the content and constructing the environment, armed as they are with the requisite understanding of psychological and cognitive readiness. The focus here, again, is on the quality of student learning. The second observation is that, within any given class, there are different students with different levels of cognitive capacity and readiness. This brings us to the next (closely related) idea of "personalized learning."

PERSONALIZED LEARNING

While student-centered learning is a fairly general term that can cover a lot of ground, personalized learning tends to focus more directly on the individual learning needs of each student. The obvious but long-coming revelation is that different students learn differently, so educators need to adjust their instructional strategies to account for this. Again, the easiest way to get at the heart of this is to see that the movement toward "personalized learning" is a reaction against the "one-size-fits-all" mentality of the Dominant model.[12]

Advocates of personalized learning usually recommend at least three component pieces to their instructional universe: the creation of flexible learning environments (where students have options about the pace and format of learning); the creation of individualized learning paths (where different students pursue different learning threads on the basis of ability and interest); and the subsequent creation of learning profiles that track achievement. The use of technology to customize instruction and monitor progress usually looms large in personalized learning models.

Many versions of personalized learning also include a fourth element: a focus on competency-based instruction wherein students must master a (usually) rudimentary set of concepts or operations in order to proceed to the next level. These are typically accessed via online programs. In the United States, these concepts or operations often match the Common Core Standards that have now become ubiquitous within that system. The perceived advantage of transporting these elements (or standards) onto an online platform is that students can work through them independently at their own pace. The software programs also automatically track student progress, thereby allowing teachers to monitor learning gaps and successes.

Blended learning, another term that parents and educators are now encountering, is simply the operational mechanism meant to enable personalized learning to be effective. It is the name given to that group of strategies that blends and incorporates online learning elements with regular classroom instruction. It includes consideration of the optimum time, format, and supervision arrangements for various instructional configurations. In at least one respected characterization, blended learning is also meant to include operational support for competency-based learning.[13] I will have more to say about blended learning later in the book.

The key feature of personalized learning that makes it a distinctive subset of student-centered learning in general is its commitment to meeting the learning needs of individual students. This concentrated focus on the instructional needs of individual learners is long overdue. As Todd Rose so clearly illustrated, the "one-size-fits-all" model does a grave disservice to our children. There is therefore significant potential to do remarkable things with students by creating more flexible learning environments that offer individualized pathways to a variety of intellectual and creative pursuits. The prospect of being able to create more sophisticated profiles of student learning is also quite tantalizing.

That said, there are again a number of elements within the domain of personalized learning about which we need to be cautious.

The use of online software platforms to facilitate competency-based learning, for example, presents the same risks we encountered in reviewing the Dominant model of education: the danger, once again, of having students acquire a set of isolated facts or operations without creating any opportunity to understand these in a larger context. While there are ways to overcome this objection, the warning for the time being is that if this is all we provide for our students, we run the risk of simply encouraging a (now digitally enhanced) rote memorization of forgettable facts to the detriment of understanding.

A second caution about personalized learning has to do with its potential to become so individualized and insular that it might very well cut students off from another rich source of learning and growth: collaborative and interdependent investigations with others.

Just as Google and Facebook are individualizing and therefore narrowing our exposure to ideas, so too might a misuse of personalized learning increase intellectual and perhaps social isolation on the part of our students. This potential pitfall can be easily guarded against by making provision for complementary educational exchanges including, for example, collaborative projects and guided class discussions. The point is that we need to make sure that personalized learning does not become so personalized that it narrows, rather than deepens, individual learning.

A final observation about personalized learning is that it focuses almost exclusively on questions of instructional technique while remaining relatively silent on questions of educational purpose. Put differently, its purposes are implicitly assumed and regarded as non-controversial, i.e., that the central focus of schools should be on enhancing student learning, whatever form that happens to take. As powerful and important as the project of individualizing learning might be, parents and educators alike still need to ask, "What learning and for what purpose?"

THE SEDUCTION OF "SKILLS"

There is a lot of enthusiasm within the Ascendant model of education for having "skills" become an essential part of the contemporary curriculum. Some would even hold that the teaching of "skills" now ought to take pride of place over knowledge acquisition as the centrepiece of a quality education. As is usual within the educational community, many different people seem to have many different ideas about what they mean by these "skills" and how exactly they are meant to contribute to an overall education. Some would suggest, for example, that because students can now look up virtually anything on the internet, schools now need to shift their emphasis to teaching students how to "learn how to learn." Others propose that there are now new sets of "21st century skills"—like design thinking and systems thinking—that contemporary citizens need as part of their toolkit to prosper. Still others think that "collaboration" and "leadership" skills need to become paramount within modern schools. Here are two example lists from a couple of typical "skills" enthusiasts:

Education 2020[14]
- Critical thinking skills (problem-solving, research, analysis, project management)
- Creativity skills (new knowledge creation, "best fit" design solutions, artful storytelling)
- Collaboration skills (consensus, cooperation, compromise, community-building)
- Cross-cultural understanding skills (knowledge & organizational cultures)
- Computing/ICT Literacy Skills (effective use of electronic information & knowledge tools)
- Career & Learning Self-Reliance Skills

Partnership for 21st Century Learning Skills[15, 16]
- Learning & Innovation Skills (Critical Thinking; Creativity; Communication; Collaboration)
- Information, Media & Technology Skills
- Life & Career Skills

At first glance, we might nod in approval at this change in direction. We might applaud the disappearance of the old regime in which we simply "crammed facts into students' heads" and celebrate instead the ascendancy of this brave new world in which students gain practical skills to make their way in the 21st century.

Nonetheless, there are reasons to be cautious here. The problem with skills language is that, if left unchecked, it can divert us away from the fullest realization of what education could be. The current infatuation with 21st century learning skills rests, in fact, on a number of mistakes and confusions that need to be addressed if we are ever going to understand and employ skills in the service of education.[17]

The first mistake involves a failure to understand how this whole general shift in favour of skills rests on a faulty conclusion drawn from the critique of traditional education. The problem with so-called "factory" schools is not that they wanted to introduce students to a whole array of substantive content. The problem was that they did this in such an amateur and ham-fisted way that whole generations came to regard the study of math, science, history, literature, and philosophy as necessary penances to be endured and then quickly forgotten. Schools within the Dominant model hardly ever connected the dots by showing students the contribution that factual knowledge makes to the achievement of understanding.

Factual knowledge is like the ingredients in a cake. You can't make a cake unless you have those ingredients, but the point is to make a cake. Sugar, eggs, salt, and flour may not be very interesting in and of themselves. What is interesting is how we can combine them together to make something wonderful. The cake, therefore, is the "explanatory framework" or the "grand concept" that unites the various parts into an interesting whole. It yields understanding. The facts are the constituent parts.

The problem with the Dominant "factory school" model is that it had students identify and memorize things like sugars, eggs, salts, and flour but never showed them how to make cakes. The problem with the Ascendant model's infatuation with skills, on the other hand, is that it focuses on the processes of food production—mixing, stirring, whipping, baking—without, again, showing students the all-important relationship between ingredients and the big picture.

The solution is not to jettison a substantive introduction to literature, mathematics, science, history, politics, philosophy, and art and completely replace these with "collaboration skills" or "critical thinking skills" or "cross-cultural understanding skills" or "career and learning self-reliance skills." The solution is instead to find a better way to introduce students to those great conversations as one foundational component to make the world more intelligible. This is not to say that the acquisition of certain kinds of skills should never be addressed within a person's education; rather, it is to say that the acquisition of skills is a second-order undertaking that needs to be subservient to the pursuit of understanding.

The second mistake occurs when we use the word "skill" to effectively reduce, dilute, and fundamentally misunderstand important educational aspirations. Take, for example, our near universal interest in "critical thinking." Almost everyone in education likes to claim that they are giving students "critical thinking skills" as part—and perhaps even as the centerpiece—of their curriculum. The popular conceit seems to be that if we give our students "critical thinking skills," they will go out into the world and be able to "think critically" about all manner of things. The truth, however, is far more complicated—and interesting—than that.

The key confusion is to assume that any set of "thinking skills"—critical thinking, creative thinking, design thinking, lateral thinking—can be taught as generic techniques that can be applied across multiple domains. But thinking always occurs within the context of some activity or field of investigation.

Imagine a student whose sole educational experience consists of participation in critical thinking and creative thinking workshops (along with various workshops on collaboration, communication, leadership, etc.). Now imagine that this person is hired to work in a physics lab—or an engineering firm, or a university English literature department. What could this person reasonably contribute? If they do not know anything about physics or mathematics or English Literature, all the critical and creative thinking courses in the world will not help them.

The truth is that we do not do anyone a service by pretending that we can teach students "critical thinking skills" in isolation from substantive content. While I think that mini-workshops in the basics of argument (and perhaps the foundations of moral reasoning) might offer some useful aids to coherent thinking, the ability to "think critically" must ultimately be grounded in substantive understanding within a particular intellectual or creative domain.[18]

A third mistake has to do with a whole set of skills that revolve around working with others (e.g., "collaboration" skills, "team-building" skills, "communication" skills and, occasionally, "leadership skills"). While the ability to work well in a group is valuable in itself, it is not actually a skill. The real problem here is our failure to distinguish a skill from a disposition.

A skill is a competency acquired over time (usually through repetition), whereas a disposition is a personal habit acquired via experience (which may have included external instruction, advice, or even admonishments). Dispositions are not really the kinds of things you can "teach," at least not in the same way you might teach a skill. Dispositions are the kind of things that need to be cultivated through a combination of intentional habits, shared experience, and compelling reasons. They are importantly different than skills.

There is nothing wrong with wanting to cultivate dispositions. Indeed, developing worthwhile dispositions is one necessary element of a complete education. Consider, for example, the dispositional elements that might be required to arrive at something we might be prepared to call critical thinking. We could start with a standard list of what used to be called intellectual virtues (for example, respect for truth, persistence, curiosity, humility). To these might be added the courage of a Galileo or a Jackson Pollock to explore new possibilities in the face of prevailing opinion.

While I do not doubt that there may be some potentially useful strategies and techniques that can be taught under the description of "Collaboration Skills" or "Communication Skills," I think it is nonetheless imperative that we understand that there are profound dispositions—virtues, if you will—that are embedded within much of our talk about skills. In understanding this, we need to appreciate that teaching skills is different from cultivating dispositions and that both of these are most appropriately an addition to—not a replacement for—the investigation of factual knowledge in the service of understanding.

Although it is indeed true that we can look up almost anything we want on the internet, the real issue is knowing what to look for. The challenge for 21st century learners is the same challenge that has faced all of our fore-bears: we need to create the capacity to ask the right questions. Having this capacity is not the kind of thing that can be acquired through special classes on "question-asking skills." It is instead a kind of wisdom and discernment that comes from having a deep and rich reservoir of knowledge and experi-ence.

WE ARE *WHERE* EXACTLY?

As indicated, even though we are in the process of moving away from the Dominant Model of education, elements of that system still remain, includ-ing age-based groupings, standardized class schedules, comparative assess-ments, and...bells. And even though there are many elements within the emerging Ascendant Model that represent promising improvements, we need to be careful to tread lightly. Our commitment to student-centered learning, for example, might have the effect of narrowing the scope of expe-riences our students have to make sense of the world. Our focus on person-alized learning could deteriorate into a simple digital progression of isolated standards to be ingested and then forgotten. And our over-emphasis on skills could deny our kids access to more profound understanding.

So, where we are, exactly, is at a crossroads—a changing of the guard. We are in the transition period between ushering out an old system and em-bracing something new. It is an unsettling time because we are being forced to break away from established patterns, but it is also an exciting time be-cause the possibilities are limitless. We are going to need all the vigilance and wisdom we can muster to ensure that we expose our students and chil-dren to something that is worthy of their time and attention.

The education radical Ivan Illich once famously wrote that "schools are the advertising agency which make you believe that you need society as it is."[19] His solution was to "de-school society"—in other words, get rid of schools. I am more optimistic. I think that we now have in our hands—perhaps for the first time ever—the ideas, resources, and technology to build a completely new model of grade-school education that can deliver on our most profound aspirations. The key element that is missing is that all-important clarity of purpose that will enable us to be intelligent and intentional about how we deploy those ideas, resources, and technologies in the service of our goals. It is time, in other words, to consider the why before how for the education of this next generation.

The Heart of The Matter

Why Before How

As it was with Island Pacific School, so too must it be in imagining a reconstituted education system for the next generation. We need to start with understanding the core purpose of the undertaking. Public and private schools alike need to start with "why before how" for at least four reasons.

First, a clear understanding of core purpose enables us to more effectively marshal our financial resources to bring about the desired ends. Educational funding will always be in high demand. It is incumbent on us that we understand precisely where we are going and why if we expect to deserve the financial support we get. This is as true for public education as it is for private and independent schools.

Second, having clarity about core purposes allows us, paradoxically enough, to be remarkably free to innovate in ways that we might not have even imagined. When we do not have a clear sense of a vision, we are more likely to passively accept the status quo and content ourselves with tinkering around the edges. If we have a clear and robust clarity of purpose, on the other hand, we are free to look at any and all things. Clarity of purpose is the royal road to intelligent innovation.

Third, we are going to need a strong hand on the tiller when it comes to navigating change, particularly with regard to educational technology. It is easy to get swept up in the enthusiasm for the most recent gizmo. When 3D printers came out, every school had to have one, never mind how they fit into particular instructional purposes. At the time of this writing, virtual reality goggles are becoming the next big thing. What is most important, however, is not the technology we use in our classrooms, but how it may (or may not) support the purposes we want to achieve. Technology does not embody or drive educational purpose. Technology is a tool that can and should be used to leverage and enhance what we want to accomplish in educational terms.

The final and most important reason to pay close attention to the "why before how" of education is that we now stand on the threshold between a slow deconstruction of the old and an as-yet undefined reconstruction of the new. Thus, we have a precious window of opportunity to push the "reset" button and create a deeper, more powerful expression of what education could be. We will squander this opportunity, however, if we rush headlong into a new implicit default that bypasses any examination of purpose and unwittingly commits us to a new version of the mediocre.

WHY BEFORE HOW WRIT LARGE

The initial clarion call at Island Pacific School to "initiate students into the great conversations of human inquiry so they can find their own voice" was a close, but ultimately imperfect, approximation of where we should be heading. Initiating students into great conversations is obviously only one element within a complete education. Likewise, "finding one's voice" doesn't capture the totality of the project. I found myself continually looking for a deeper and richer rendering of the essential purpose of not only our school, but of the three levels of grade school—elementary, middle, and secondary—as a whole.

After over twenty years mulling it over, I think the best candidate I can offer is this: *the essential purpose of education, and our fundamental job as educators, is to help equip and inspire students to cultivate their humanity.*

Although this notation is short, it is meant to encapsulate both philosophical and operational ideas. The philosophical issue centers on what it might mean to "cultivate humanity." The operational question is what it would look like to "equip and inspire" students for such a formidable purpose.

CULTIVATING HUMANITY

The phrase "cultivating humanity" comes from the title of a book by Martha Nussbaum[1] about university education. The central idea is that human beings have certain capacities—powers, if you will—including the ability to reason; to see things from a moral point of view; to be expressive and creative; to be intentional about our physicality; to appreciate art, music, and literature; and to think about our thinking, and the point of life is to cultivate these powers as a personal expression of the very best of what it is to be a human being.

This idea has a strong historical lineage, for it represents the classical ideal of a liberal education. First formulated in ancient Greece, the central question was, "What sort of education would enable a person to be free?" For the Greeks, this meant the kind of education that would be appropriate for a free Greek citizen. However, subsequent commentary on liberal education has attempted to express what "freedom" might mean for human beings in general.

In *Beyond the Present and Particular: A Theory of Liberal Education*, Cambridge professor Charles Bailey offers a double formulation of "freedom" within the context of liberal education—both "freedom from" the ignorance and superstitions of one's time and "freedom for" the fullest expression of the very best of what it is to be a human being.[2]

The educational project needed to address "freedom from" is relatively straightforward. Students need, at the very least, a strong grounding in history, science, and perhaps contemporary rhetoric if they are not going to be mere pawns within what Charles Bailey calls the "tyranny of their times."

The idea of education grounded in some conception of "freedom for" the fullest expression of the best of who we are, however, is more difficult to articulate because it requires an antecedent declaration of this notion of the "best" of what it is to be a human being. In the contemporary world, we tend to be wary of identifying any single "best"; we prefer to proclaim that there are multiple "bests," and even that one "best" is as good as another.

This reticence rests on an inability, I think, to appreciate the distinction between the legitimate acknowledgement of individual aspirations and our collective endorsement of the representative accomplishments of the species as a whole. As a species we have eradicated smallpox, landed on the moon, created breathtaking art, condemned slavery and child labour, and found a way to change our political leadership without bloodshed. We are even starting to figure out our moral obligations to other sentient beings. These are human accomplishments; they represent us at our best.

But there is a second, more contemporary, obligation within education that extends beyond introducing students to the depth and breadth of human achievement. This is the idea that education must, in some way, help individuals to discover and develop their own unique interests and capacities, i.e., their "own voice." When parents want "happiness" for their children, part of what they mean is they want them to have the opportunity to find and follow their true passions. This is a distinctly modern expectation that surpasses the medieval sensibility that one should be content in fulfilling their preordained role in society. Our contemporary hope for our children is, in part, that they find meaning in their lives by pursuing and expressing their own particular gifts.

The Greek poet Pindar unwittingly offers us the best expression of the ideal combination of classical and contemporary educational purposes. His famous clarion call to his contemporaries was to "Become what you are." While this phrase can become misinterpreted within a modern context to mean something like "follow your bliss," Pindar's classical formulation would have focused more on the potential of human beings—as human beings—to express the very best of who we are as a species.

Pindar's subsequent question, "How ought one to live?" provides the key to combining the classical and the contemporary. On one hand, we might answer the question by saying our responsibility is to cultivate our distinctly human powers so as to express, contribute to, and participate in the very best of what it is to be a human being. This is the classical formulation. On the other hand, we might say that our aim in life is to discover and develop our unique interests, abilities, and passions—in other words, our calling—which is the contemporary perspective. If education is about cultivating humanity, we need to set students up to intentionally pursue both formulations.

More precisely, we need to see that the pursuit and expression of individual passion—of individual excellence—is best understood and evaluated in the context of the larger human narrative.

What do I mean by that? Isaac Newton once said, "If I have seen further, it is by standing on the shoulders of giants." He meant that his ideas need to be understood in the context of the scientific explorations of the people who came before him. On the island where I live, there is a heavy machinery driver who is an absolute artist when it comes to building rock retaining walls. Recognized and celebrated as a local master of this, he must take some satisfaction from the fact that his skill is compared and located within the abilities of his colleagues, and indeed within the broader human enterprise of deftly manipulating our physical environment.

The invitation to "cultivate our humanity," therefore, has a triple meaning. It means we should strive to express the very best of what it is to be a human being—for example, to develop our powers to reason, to be expressive and creative, to be intentional about our health and physicality, to think about our thinking, and to be moral agents. It also means we should strive to discover and develop our own unique interests, abilities, and passions—our calling. Finally, it means we should eventually understand and appreciate how our own interests, abilities, and talents are part of a larger human narrative, or "great conversation."

EQUIP AND INSPIRE

As educators, it is a tall order indeed to actively equip and inspire students to pursue these purposes. What would that look like? Although I will offer my own rough template of a grade 10-12 program later in the book, here is a preliminary list of the kinds of things that might need to be included:

- A thorough grounding in "emancipatory competencies"—those basic understandings and skills that "free" students to fully engage and participate within contemporary society. While reading and basic numeracy are perhaps the most obvious candidates, this also includes a capacity to understand and produce arguments and an ability to produce relevant and thoughtful answers to questions.

- A meaningful initiation into "the great conversations of human inquiry." In order to understand how one's personal interests or calling might resonate within a larger human narrative, students need some introductory picture of what that larger narrative might be. They need, therefore, at least an initial familiarity with those remarkable conversations in science, art, philosophy, sport, literature, religion, and technology that human beings have conducted over the past 5,000 years. The challenge will be to make this initiation truly meaningful in the context of each student's life.

- A progression of individual and group opportunities for students to pursue questions and projects of personal interest. These might include everything from mini-explorations of bugs, dinosaurs, catapults, unicorns—whatever the kids are interested in—right up to full Masterworks investigations whereby students acquire comprehensive understanding and a kind of mastery of their topic.

- A set of carefully-crafted personal challenges that will, over time, build *warranted* confidence. While these might take many forms—overcoming stage fright, facing insurmountable odds on a rugby pitch, completing a particularly arduous outdoor hike—the point is that they need to be genuine challenges in order to ensure that the resultant confidence is legitimately earned.

- At least one experience, and hopefully several, where a student is removed from his or her immediate cultural experience and is compelled—through temporary immersion in another—to see things from a different perspective. The possibilities here are limitless: spending a day in a wheelchair, attending a religious service outside one's own beliefs, being exposed to music or art that extends beyond current one's tastes, creating a relationship with a digital pen pal from another culture, visiting and working within a neighbourhood that is different from one's own.

- A progression of opportunities for students to make a positive contribution to the communities in which they reside. One of the best experiences for our middle school students was to spend a couple of hours a month reading to preschool students down the road. In any community, there are always plenty of opportunities to lend a hand and make a difference.

- An explicit invitation to cultivate those dispositions or virtues that are necessary for the fullest expression of the very best of what it is to be a human being. These would include such "intellectual virtues" as care and attention to detail, fidelity to the truth, humility, a capacity to change one's mind on the basis of better reasons, and a respectful reticence to change one's mind unless given compelling reasons to do so. They would also include more general virtues like curiosity, honesty, self-awareness, integrity of word, and compassion.

- An ongoing exposure to human excellence that will include real-time exposure to contemporary exemplars of human curiosity and expression. A regular "Featured Speakers" series involving artists, scientists, politicians, entrepreneurs, and the like might be augmented with screened TED Talks dealing with all manner of ideas and innovations.

Even though these general descriptors admit of a broad range of possibilities, it is important to see that they also rule out certain approaches to education. What is decidedly not being proposed here is any *laissez faire* model in which the tastes and desires of the student become the sole driver of what is to be learned. Nor is there any slavish memorization of inert cultural artifacts separated out from an explanatory narrative. There is instead an attempt here to expose students to a set of experiences and give them the tools they need to recognize and nurture the best of what it is to be a human being and, within that context, to discover and develop their own interests, abilities, and passions.

DEEP PROSPERITY

In framing the aims and program elements of education in this way, I am proposing that we recapture the public purpose of schooling in what we do with students. This requires that we better understand both the personal and public benefits of education and how they are related.

The most fundamental personal benefit of education is that, when properly conducted, it creates the conditions to enable individuals to discover and express those capacities that are unique to the human species—our creativity, our curiosity, and our compassion. We gain the ability to, in Pindar's words, "become what we are." The more specific personal benefit is that it creates the opportunity to discover and develop our own distinctive strengths and interests. In gaining exposure to a broad range of experiences and narratives, we eventually come to see which of these will take hold to capture our commitment and imagination. In doing so, we come to define a part of our life that gives us meaning.

The public benefit of education is best appreciated by a careful consideration of what are sometimes called "neighbourhood effects." The basic idea is that what happens in schools affects not only the individuals involved but also the "neighbourhood" as a whole—not simply the immediate neigh-bourhood in the vicinity of the school but the very fabric of our society. The proposition here is that if we create the conditions in schools to enable our youth to acquire baseline literacy competencies, become introduced to the great conversations of human inquiry, cultivate a moral sensibility based on respect for persons, and discover and develop their unique interests and abilities, we enrich our society as a whole.

These are not purposes that follow a utilitarian rationale that would simply train and socialize students to operate within society as it is currently con-figured. Nor are they exclusively technical by focusing on "best practices" for teaching and learning without considering the aims these practices are meant to serve. These purposes are practical and aspirational in nature. They are practical in that they enable students to operate within a world that may be radically different from the one we know today. They are aspi-rational because they encourage students to locate their personal interests in the context of a larger narrative of collective well-being.

These purposes, moreover, are ultimately directed to what might best be called "deep prosperity." This is not the prosperity that champions self-interest at the expense of others but seeks instead to activate the capacity of individuals to express they very best of who they are. This is the kind of prosperity that encourages and enables us to take our humanity up a notch.

To propose that the essential purpose of education—and our fundamental job as educators—is to "equip and inspire students to cultivate their human-ity" is to set a very high bar. But it seems to me that if we aspire to anything less than this, we will fall into the trap of simply re-inventing the same old wheel or unwittingly accepting a new status quo that once again aims too low. If we begin with powerful purposes, however, anything is possible.

Structure Matters

Bring in the Architects

It is one thing to propose a philosophical clarion call for a transformed grade school education system writ large; it is quite another to specify the operational moves that need to be made to deliver on that promise.

I have a good friend who is a public school principal and to whom I periodically let fly my aspirations for a better way of doing things. While she is polite and occasionally sympathetic to some of my ideas, more often than not she can barely conceal her frustration and annoyance. She is frustrated because she works within a system that has significant structural constraints on what she can and cannot do as an educator. We talked once, for example, about the benefit of having middle school students of a particular age separated out from the elementary and high school cohorts. She pointed out that such pedagogical considerations were pretty much irrelevant, given that the school board makes (changing) decisions about school configurations on the basis of population changes and economic efficiency. She was annoyed with my numerous philosophical speculations because she understood that hardly any of these could come to fruition within the system as it currently stood. While I had the luxury of being able to create my own school (more or less) according to my own specifications, she did not. More to the point, the structural components of my school—small class sizes, small school size—were effectively irrelevant to a public system of education that needed to serve a large population of learners across a broad spectrum of abilities.

I therefore understand my friend's frustration and annoyance as a public school principal who, like many of her colleagues, strives mightily every day to do the best she can, given the conditions she faces and the resources she has at her disposal.

I confess to feeling the same kind of frustration and annoyance when I hear certain educational luminaries offering their now obvious critiques of contemporary education and then extolling us (in the same way I have done in the previous chapter) to choose a better path. The problem—and the frustration—is that we have only presented a cup half full. When it comes to education, as with most things, you can have all the ideas in the world, but if you do not have the means to bring them about, these aspirations will not amount to anything but, as my grandmother used to say, "a hill of beans."

In a recent article about educational reform in the Harvard Business Review[1], the authors looked at 411 leaders of academies in the UK and identified five types of leadership approaches regarding school improvement, including that of the "Accountant," the "Architect," the "Philosopher," the "Soldier," and the "Surgeon." They then revealed one of these as being the most effective in terms of bringing about improvement according to their specified criteria: exam scores and the financial health of the school over time.

According to the authors, the "Accountant" is the educational leader who tries to grow their schools out of trouble by looking for new revenue sources, such as acquiring a primary school or developing non-teaching revenue streams (summer rentals, etc.). The "Architect" is the leader who redesigns the school to create the right environment for its teachers and the right school for its community. The "Philosopher" is the person who is "passionate about teaching" and believes schools fail "because they are not teaching their students properly." The "Soldier" likes efficiency and order and tends to see running a school as similar to managing a large IT project, where a focus on costs and deadlines will allow the rest to take care of itself. And the "Surgeon" quickly identifies what's not working and redirects resources to the most pressing problem (which, in this case, is exam results). Surgeons are, according to the authors, "tough, disciplined leaders who believe that their job is to get the school back in shape fast with new rules and hard work."[2]

Putting aside for a moment the core assumptions of the study (that "effective" leaders are those that generate good exam results and a healthy bottom line), which one do you think was the most effective?

Accountants do indeed improve the bottom line, but exam results stay more or less the same. Surgeons improve exam results while they are there, but exam scores fall back to where they started after they leave because younger students have been ignored and under-resourced for the interim years. Soldiers improve financial performance while they are there, but this fades when they leave. They also do not noticeably increase test scores, and they create a climate of fear uncertainty amongst staff that can take years to repair. And philosophers, apparently, fare the worst in terms of school improvement understood in these terms. The authors claim that while "they talk a good game, [they] have no impact." Their performance, in terms of finance and examination results, stays the same.

The architects, however, take a long-term view of what they need to do and then combine the best parts of the other leaders to focus on the main task: transforming students and communities. "They take a 360-degree view of the school, its stakeholders, the community it serves, and its role in society."[3] Although performance is slow to improve, they eventually get enhanced examination results that continue to improve long after they've left. "They are visionary, unsung heroes. Stewards rather than leaders, who are more concerned with the legacy they leave than how things look whilst they're there."[4]

As someone who has most definitely come at education from a philosophical point of view, and who has enjoyed "debating and discussing alternative teaching methods" with teachers (a practice the authors include in their description of the ineffective philosopher), I must confess to initially being taken aback by their analysis. As mentioned previously, I think it is crucially important to "invite teachers to become educators" in the sense of engaging them in a thoughtful conversation about the essential purpose of education and how they might contribute to this profoundly important project. It is also worth making the philosophical point that increased examination scores and an improved bottom line are imperfect proxies, at best, for the architect's apparent goal to "transform students and communities."

All of that said, I think the authors of this research are nonetheless onto something very important: it is not good enough to be merely philosophical about education; we need to take an architectural approach as well.

In a public presentation entitled "How to Change Education From the Ground Up",[5] educational author and commentator Ken Robinson talks a very good philosophical game, indeed, but comes up short on the architectural changes that need to be made in order to deliver on the dream. After a thoughtful introduction wherein he proposes that the "basics" we need to pay attention to in education are its essential purposes (i.e., why before how), he offers a critique of top-down management and then moves on to propose that, if we really want education to be effective, what we most need to focus on is the process of teaching and learning. Good teachers, he thinks, "need to be able to excite people, find points of entry, engage them, fuel their creativity, drive their passion." When someone asked, "but how can you do that with 35 kids in a classroom?" his retort was that he has known teachers who have 42 kids in a class, and they were all engaged. His advice was that you do not engage students by teaching them but by getting them actively involved.

While perhaps temporarily inspirational, this is a tad simplistic. Even though it is no doubt true that some teachers may have managed to get 42 students "engaged" for at least some portion of a class, it is more universally true that there are real structural constraints for most teachers to bring about this level of engagement across an entire system of education as currently constructed.

A little later on in his presentation, Robinson makes a direct appeal to teachers by saying that "if you are in that [all important teacher-learner] relationship, then 'you hold the tools of power right in your hand'"; in other words, "you can change the system by yourself."[6]

This kind of public proposition is problematic and borders on irresponsible. It is problematic because the operational constraints that real teachers (and real school leaders) are operating under are significant. It is not simply a matter of class size; it is bigger than that. We have teachers teaching subjects they know little or nothing about within a standardized delivery and assessment system that is trying to reach students of wildly different levels of ability and interest. Real teachers teaching in real classrooms understand that they live within a world of constant compromise.

This kind of proposition borders on irresponsibility, moreover, because it leads to guilt, defeat, and cynicism when teachers are predictably unable to deliver on the dream. Guilt comes for those teachers who genuinely want to have an impact on all their students. They struggle heroically to excite people, find points of entry, engage them, fuel their creativity, and drive their passion, and they also look for ways to have their students "get actively involved" instead of teaching them directly. While they will have their successes, to be sure, the more perceptive of them will see that there are systemic roadblocks that bar the way to the kind of breakthrough they are looking for. This might take the form of a restrictive job evaluation format, or a lack of adequate student support, or an assessment system that focuses on the wrong things. If they stay in the profession long enough, they are then liable to defeat and cynicism. In the absence of any systemic structural change, they will get tired of beating their heads against a wall and will re-treat instead into self-survival mode.

Robinson finishes off his presentation by attempting to evoke a social "movement" that would change education from the ground up. He believed (in 2013 when he made this presentation) that the "revolution" had already begun, and he cited the use of iPads in schools in Austin, Texas and the rise of MOOCs[7] as evidence of this.

What my public school principal friend and the authors of the school leader-ship study tell me, however, is that education cannot be transformed by merely philosophically wishing it so, or by hoping that a "movement" will emerge. This time around we desperately need architects—as well as phi-losophers—to put ideas into action. The philosophers, like Robinson, do indeed need to prod us on essential questions of purpose, but the architects need to show us in detail how exactly we might deliver on our dreams.

In the second half of the book, I am going to concentrate on structural, or "architectural," issues. While much of what I have to say will be of direct relevance to teachers and educational leaders, this section is also crucially important for parents as well. If parents are going to be active and informed partners in shaping their children's learning—as I believe they should be—they need to better understand the challenges and opportunities that teachers and administrators face in trying to provide this next generation with the best education possible.

Structure Matters

Back to the Drawing Board

The proposition here is that, even with the best intentions in the world, we are not going to be able to create an education system that enables students to "cultivate their humanity" (at least, not in the manner I have suggested) unless we are prepared to fundamentally re-engineer our entire way of doing things. We need to re-examine all the component parts of our current model, keeping those elements that work, redesigning others, and discarding those that need to go. We need, in other words, to go back to the drawing board.

Consider, for example, this one-line description of the standard practices within the dominant model of education:

> *Teachers teach a defined curriculum, in a unified way, to single age instructional groups, of a defined size, in a defined space, over a defined time, within a defined schedule.*

The good news is that this is not a completely accurate description of the current state of affairs in most contemporary schools. We have already made some promising changes to some of these elements. The truth, however, is that if we want to create the kind of education that successfully incorporates personalized learning, for example, as one element within a larger educational program, we still have more work to do. Perhaps the best way to see this is to start by listing some of the initial questions that naturally arise when considering each separate component within that descriptive sentence above:

teachers teach	Does it only have to be a "teacher" who "teaches" students? Can other people (other adults, peers) interact with them in educationally productive ways? What place do online learning platforms have in the delivery of a comprehensive educational program?
a defined curriculum	How should a "curriculum" be understood? As a series of courses to be completed, or as something larger than this? Should it be precisely prescribed or more like a framework?
in a unified way	What operational structures need to be in place to enable teachers, or the system as a whole, to offer *truly* personalized instruction that is tuned to different learning styles and abilities? How can teachers, and the education system as a whole, avoid the great compromise where no-one really gets what they need?
single age groups	Why do we always have to arrange educational experiences for students within single age groups? Which elements are best arranged in single age groups and which might be better arranged in multi-aged cohorts?
defined size	Does class size matter? What sizes of learning groups are most amenable to which kinds of learning activities? How do we better leverage learning in microgroups of, say, one to five?

defined space	Are classrooms, as currently arranged, the best places to learn things? Can we configure classrooms different-ly? Can we design schools differently with multiple learning spaces?
defined time	Do all lessons, or learning episodes, need to happen within the same timeframe? How do we best address the reality that different students take different amounts of time to reap the benefits of different kinds of learning experiences?
defined schedule	Is there a way to design an instructional schedule that makes best use of teachers and other instructional pro-viders, while at the same time being flexible enough to be responsive to the learning needs of individual learn-ers?

Let's have a closer look at each of these elements as well as a few others to see how we might start to think differently about other possible futures for grade school education.

TEACHERS

Teachers currently do all kinds of things: prepare and teach lessons, prepare and grade tests and assignments, provide instructional support to students (where they can), manage and discipline students, encourage and inspire them, supervise lunch and excursions, complete report cards, participate in parent conferences, run clubs or coach sports, and attend planning and pro-fessional development workshops. Within their instructional purview in par-ticular, they are expected to teach their subjects in a way that takes proper account of developmental capabilities so that students can demonstrate competence in the essentials of the study, all the while being actively and enthusiastically engaged in the subject matter. They are expected, in other words, to be part child psychologist, part content expert, and part cheer-leader.

Naturally enough, they do some of these things well and some of them poorly. On one hand, they can be masters at knowing which students need what kind of support, while on the other, they can seriously misunderstand the fundamentals of the subject matter they are teaching. They can create great learning experiences for their students but be negligent when it comes to their supervision. And, like most people, they enjoy some parts of their job and find other parts painful.

Here's a potential pivot question: what parts of a teacher's job could be better managed in some other fashion, for example by an online learning program or someone other than a teacher?

In 2015, the staff at Island Pacific School ran a series of blended learning pilot projects in which they tried to incorporate some element of online learning within their overall instructional plan. While different projects met with different levels of success, the general take-away for us was that there is huge potential to incorporate some elements of online learning within a total educational program. Indeed, it is now obvious that online learning is already becoming an important core component of contemporary educational delivery. The real trick, of course, is to determine which elements of online learning are best incorporated where, and for what purpose. The question, insofar as teacher responsibilities are concerned, is how their particular expertise might best be deployed within an overall educational program.

It is relevant to note, for example, that some teachers are particularly good at understanding the specific learning needs of individual students, while others are ingenious about making the subject matter come alive for students. Are these two separate roles? Are some people more suited to finding ways to support students as individual learners, while others are masters of curriculum development borne perhaps out of a passion for the subject matter? If so, what are the implications for how we structure teaching jobs?

And what about the option of having people other than teachers take on some portion of a teacher's responsibilities? When we ran the Masterworks program at Island Pacific School, we had people in the community (and beyond) serve as external advisors on the students' advisory committees. We could not have run the program without them; we did not have the personnel. More to the point, we wanted and needed external advisors precisely because they had something we lacked: particular knowledge and experience or passion for the project under investigation. The upside was significant: we were able to get our students to interact with adults on a topic of shared interest, and the external advisors were delighted to share their expertise with the next generation. The potential for similar kinds of learning exchanges and mini-apprenticeships is enormous. It takes a village indeed.

The overall challenge is to find those opportunities to restructure the responsibilities of teachers in a way that will leverage their particular expertise and the quality of the educational system as a whole. People are interested in, and good at, different things. Just as we want to personalize learning for our students, so too might we find ways to personalize the jobs of our teachers. Some people are great at teaching grammar, and others are not. Some understand what makes students tick, while others are brilliant at making subject matter accessible. The challenge is to see if we can create a system in which the right person ends up in the right job.

CURRICULUM

Our current practice is to define "curriculum" in terms of a series of subject areas—math, science, English, "social studies" (in some form), second language, physical education, art—that need in some way to be addressed. In the middle and high school years, these subjects—and all the skill requirements, tests, and assignments associated with them—are shoehorned into a set of courses that need to be completed. We also have any number of "extra-curricular" activities within schools that are considered apart from the formal "academic" curriculum. Is this the best way to think about the programs and experiences that students encounter in schools?

Isn't it the case that some of the most profound and important learning happens via some of those extra-curricular activities? And is it true that everything associated with academic learning has to happen within the context of a course? Are there important and substantive components of what we want in our curriculum that we can more beneficially approach in different ways?

And how, moreover, might we start to see curriculum less as a set of prescribed courses and more as an open framework designed to meet foundational purposes?

In the Possible Futures section that follows, I will propose that we need to start thinking about the full range of program elements (rather than just courses) that we want to include in our curriculum. I will even offer a description of what some of these elements might look like for high school. I will also offer a few thoughts about the advantages of "open" versus "closed" systems of education. For the moment, though, it is enough to ask whether we might be better served by a deeper and richer understanding of curriculum.

INSTRUCTION

Modern technology has the capacity to enhance learning in at least two ways. First, the internet offers classroom teachers an incredibly rich diversity of educational resources that can make learning come alive for students. Student can now tour the Louvre,[1] manipulate the periodic table of elements,[2] dissect a frog,[3] learn math via NASA modules,[4] and do any number of other things from their computers at school. Second, increasingly sophisticated online learning platforms are capable of carrying at least some of the weight of a comprehensive educational program. Programs like the Khan

Academy, Math IXL, or Duolingo allow students to progress at their own rate and enable teachers to keep close track of successes and challenges. Some independent schools, like the AltSchools in the USA, have created even more sophisticated proprietary software that offers a playlist of learning experiences and tracks individual student progress.

The challenge for teachers and educational leaders is to figure out which resources to deploy for what purposes in the context of an overall educational architecture. There is a tendency to become infatuated with digital resources and educational technology in and of themselves, and to use them even if other more traditional methods might be more appropriate. There is also the problem of using poor quality digital resources to reproduce the worst of our past educational practices by simply giving students the equivalent of electronic worksheets.

As briefly introduced in the review of personalized learning, one approach that is making its way to the forefront of contemporary instructional practice is that of "Blended Learning." The basic idea, as the name implies, is to find the right mix between teacher-directed instruction and technology-driven or third-party learning so that students receive the best of both worlds.[5]

Following the lead of Clayton M. Christensen's work on "disruptive innovation," Michael B. Horn and Heather Staker have laid out the basic contours of the emerging field in their book, *Blended: Using Disruptive Innovation to Improve Schools*.[6] Their more comprehensive definition of Blended Learning emphasizes the importance of some measure of student agency within the overall learning architecture:

> *A formal education program in which a student learns at least in part through online learning with some element of student control over time, place, path, and/or pace and at least in part at a supervised brick and mortar location away from home. The modalities along each student's learning path in a course or subject are connected to provide an integrated learning experience.[7]*

In their book, Horn and Staker provide a survey of the educational landscape by offering four models of Blended Learning as follows.[8]

Rotation Model Station Rotation, Lab Rotation, Flipped Classroom, Individual Rotation	Any course or subject in which students rotate—either on a fixed schedule or at the teacher's discretion—among learning modalities, at least one of which is online learning.[9] Examples: Rocketship Education
Flex Model	Students learn via an individually customized, fluid schedule among learning modalities allowing them to alternate between online learning and face-to-face formats. Examples: AltSchool[10], Acton Academy[11]
A La Carte Model	Any course that a student takes online while also attending a brick-and-mortar school. Example: Students access a course through Global Online Academy[12], while completing other courses at a regular school.
Enriched Virtual Model	Online courses that offer required face-to-face learning sessions but allow students to do the rest of the work online from wherever they prefer. Example: Commonwealth Connections Academy[13]

They also point out, importantly, that "blended learning is different from technology-rich instruction. "With the former, students have at least some control of the time, place, path, and/or pace of their learning, whereas with the latter, the learning activities are standardized across the class."[14] Again, the emphasis in Blended Learning is on ensuring at least some measure of student agency.

The point here is that there are ways to rethink our instructional practices—and to reconfigure our entire learning environments—by, in part, intelligently incorporating digital resources into our overall educational plan. In the next section, I will offer a few contemporary examples of what this might look like.

STUDENT SUPPORT

The standard model of student support is to assume that there is a majority of so-called "normal" kids who need little to no support, and then there are other kids on both ends of the spectrum—"challenged" and "gifted"—who need significant assistance. The standard response, therefore, is to have teachers deal with the majority of students as best they can and then deploy educational assistants to help the challenged kids or create special programs for the "gifted."

But what if we started with a different working assumption? What if we assumed that all students need some level of learning support and baked this right into our educational system accordingly? Contemporary educators are now starting to speak about the various "learning profiles" of students with cognitive and/or psychological challenges. What if we assumed, right from the beginning, that everyone has their own distinctive learning profile, and that part of "equipping and inspiring" students to "cultivate their humanity" requires that we understand what makes each one of them tick? And what if we built an entire educational architecture with this in mind?

How could this happen, and what would it look like? Part of the solution, I believe, will come about by re-engineering our programs. If we can create enough opportunities for personalized learning of the defined curriculum and individual or group exploration of topics of interest, some of the support issues will evaporate. That said, there will still be students who require some level of direct support with individual studies and perhaps across the program as a whole. This latter challenge will need to be addressed by both personnel and scheduling.

The Westside School in Vancouver, British Columbia has created a special program for their grade 10-12 students that they call the Miniversity. The basic idea is that students complete one full course every five weeks (which enables them to complete the requisite 7-8 courses over an academic year). What is interesting is the way the teachers can—and do—arrange their courses knowing that they have more or less an entire day available to them every weekday, for five weeks. What usually happens is that they teach some kind of introductory focus lesson first thing in the morning, and then give the students the rest of the day to work independently or in study groups on the follow-up assignments or investigations. This creates a perfect opportunity for the teacher and/or a student learning specialist to meet with each student on a regular basis to offer them directed support. (There could be as many as 40 half-hour tutorial slots available every week.)

It is certainly a significant structural move to have high school students complete one course every five weeks. But what if the attendant payoffs were so significant that we could fundamentally change the educative experience for our students? I am not sure that having students complete courses in five-week semesters is the only, or even the best, way to create some breathing space to allow for more comprehensive student support. I am sure, however, that it will be structural changes of this magnitude that will be required to break open our current operational shell and allow us to build something significantly better.

COMPOSITION

There are all kinds of reasons why it might make sense to have students work their way through an education system in age-equivalent groups, where everyone in a learning cohort is more or less the same age. Students of the same age are thought to be more or less at the same stage of cognitive development, so it only stands to reason that they should learn in age consistent cohorts. And yet, as any experienced teacher can tell you, there is usually a fairly broad diversity of cognitive capacity within any typical classroom. We all know this because teachers routinely have to find ways to provide extra support for those students who struggle and extra challenge for those who are intellectually bored. If the cognitive diversity is too great in a classroom, as is often the case, then—in theory, if not in practice—special educational assistants are called in to ameliorate the situation.

We might also claim that age-equivalent learning cohorts are the most appropriate for general social development. Other things being equal, it makes sense for kids to socialize with others of their own age. But does it really? Is this always the case? When we first opened Island Pacific School, I had to run what I called the "three-ring circus" by having three separate grades (and ages) of students in the same classroom. While this was admittedly difficult from an operational point of view, I did notice one thing: the younger students became more thoughtful and mature in the company of their older colleagues.

Socialization can cut both ways. Several years later (when we had age-specific classes), I had a homeschooling parent make the decision not to send his son to our school because he did not want to expose him to the negative socialization that can sometimes occur amongst self-absorbed adolescents. I could see his point.

It is interesting, by the way, how accustomed we have become to making friends or finding romantic companions that are more or less our own age. During school, the age restrictions are fairly severe: one did not typically make friends with, or go out with, anyone from a different grade. After school, the acceptable age range becomes broader the older we get. We find younger and older friends, and we get into relationships with age differences that can span a decade or more. While most companionships are formed out of shared experiences which tend to involve people of more or less the same age, it is nonetheless interesting to consider how our grade school learning cohorts may have socialized us toward an unnecessary and ultimately limiting view of appropriate inter-age interactions.

I am not saying that we should restructure things such that students never do things in age-consistent cohorts, for there are enough common-sense reasons to have individuals learn many things together with people who are more or less their same age. I am saying, however, that we should look for strategic opportunities to change up age groupings for both social and educational encounters when doing so supports our broader purposes.

Having older students help tutor younger students, for example, fulfills two goals simultaneously: it provides older students with an opportunity to make a genuine contribution to others, and it provides a built-in relevance point for their own learning. Countless teachers are already aware that you don't really know something until you can explain it to others. Properly structured cross-age student mentorships are another way to make an educationally valuable connection between older and younger students.

I think the most interesting educative opportunity, however, would be to arrange things so that different-aged students get the opportunity to work together on collaborative learning projects. If these are designed in a way where students are invited to play to their own strengths and if different aged students bring different kinds of strengths to the table (as they most certainly will), we will create a clear demonstration of the things that can be done when ability, not age, becomes the criteria for participation.

I happened upon a great example of what this might look like while watching my twin daughters work as film directors. What struck me as remarkable was the way in which different individuals brought different kinds of expertise to the film set. There were directors, assistant directors, directors of photography, producers, lighting people, sound people, costume people, make-up people, location people, special effects people, key grips, best boys, and many others. While all of these people were working to complete the vision of the director(s), they each had their own specific job to do, and they did it well. And although most of the people on the set fit more or less within one generation, the age differential was still at least 10-15 years.

I do not know in what instances, and under what conditions, it will make sense to introduce cross-age learning and socialization experiences for children. This is something, again, that educational leaders and teachers will need to determine in the context of their own situation. I know that parents, for the most part, do not favour split classes, and I know how hard it was for me to run my "three ring circus" at Island Pacific School. But it is still worth asking, in reconfiguring our architecture, whether we might see some powerful benefits to creating more cross-age learning interactions amongst our students.

NUMBER

There is a lot of consternation these days about class size. People seem to think that if classes are smaller, that is automatically a good thing. Indeed, even at Island Pacific School, we highlighted the fact that our classes were relatively small (although my main focus was always on what we did in those classes). While there is much learned debate on the nuances of instructional group size, there are a couple of very obvious observations that are plain to anyone who has actually worked with students.

The first of these is that smaller class sizes create the opportunity for more individual student interactions than larger classes. By interactions, I mean both communication between teachers and students (i.e., to check for comprehension) and communication between the students themselves (i.e., in the case of a class discussion). At a very basic level, it is simply a matter of doing the math: if I have 16-18 students in my class, I have significantly more opportunity to create interactions with students than I would if I had 25-30.

But issues of class size are, of course, intimately linked to questions of use and purpose. If one's purpose is to introduce students to the norms of intelligent conversation, then groups of 12-16 are ideal. If the purpose, on the other hand, is simply to give a presentation (that might serve as a foundation piece for subsequent individual investigation), that can likely be done in larger groups. Notice that it is possible to waste the advantage of small class size by teaching in a way that would work equally well for groups of 25 and beyond. Alternatively, if you understand what you are doing and why you are doing it, a good teacher can leverage the advantages of a small group to meet educational purposes that cannot be achieved in another context.

One sometimes comes across educational research that suggests that "class size doesn't matter." What these studies usually have in mind, though, is the difference between class sizes of, for example, 20-25 and those of 25-30. The proposition is that there is not much difference in terms of student "effect" between the two.

This points to a second obvious observation that people in the field already intuitively know: there are different threshold sizes for groups that yield different instructional or interactive possibilities. It is one thing to have a group size of 16-18, another to have classes of 20-30, and quite another to have classes of 35-150. Universities already know this. That is why they will have professors present big ideas in lectures to classes of 150 (or more), and then have graduate students conduct smaller seminar sessions to work through the particulars.

There is, therefore, no ideal class size; it depends on what exactly one is trying to accomplish. Small classes can be good for interactive discussions, hands-on experiments, and supported instruction. Larger classes can be useful for big picture overviews, demonstrations, and special presentations. Moreover, to focus only on "classes" is to fail to be cognizant of the incredibly rich learning and engagement opportunities that can be arranged within the mini-constituencies of one to five students. More attention needs to be paid to the ways in which individual students, or micro-groups, can effectively "teach themselves" some of the essential elements of an overall curriculum. And, as we have seen, much more attention needs to be paid to the way that technology can augment and enhance education at the micro-level.

And quite apart from class size, there is the much less-discussed issue of school size. At present, there seems to be a default understanding where public schools of less than 120-150 students are not considered viable as stand-alone entities. This is likely due to "economy of scale" arguments having to do with things like square footage cost and breadth of program availability relative to the number of teachers required and students serviced. The question, though, is whether or not there are good educational reasons to figure out how to create and financially sustain different sizes of schools—or federations of smaller schools—for different levels of education. With 65 students in grades 6-9, Island Pacific School is admittedly an outlier. But it is an outlier that works very well. There is something to be said for seeing what we can learn from different configurations.

SPACE

A few years after we started Island Pacific School, we installed individual learner cubicles around the perimeter of the classroom walls and put a giant seminar table in the middle. Remarkably, we also gave our rambunctious middle school students "rolly chairs" (swivel chairs with wheels). The idea was that they would work independently at their cubicles and then roll up to the seminar table when we needed to discuss things as a group. Because each grade was permanently located in a separate classroom (and the teachers rotated through), the students could outfit and "decorate" their cubicles as they saw fit.

That configuration eventually disappeared as our school grew larger. Because we had more students to rotate through a finite number of classrooms, the cubicles had to go in favour of a horseshoe arrangement that could be used by multiple classes.

I have been thinking a lot lately about the importance of having form follow function. Back in the early years, our "form" of the classroom followed a number of required functions: we wanted individual spaces where kids could work on their own, a collective meeting space where we could discuss ideas as a group, and some quick mobility between the two. Hence cubicles, a seminar table, and rolly chairs.

When we made the switch later, we lost some functionality as a result of the new form. Students now have no individual workspaces, nor do they "own" their rooms. The closeness of a seminar table was made less intimate by the introduction of the open horseshoe with the teacher at a separate table in the front. While there were logistical and organizational reasons for making these changes, those reasons effectively trumped our original educative intuitions.

We have done this a lot in schools—that is, allow "logistical and organizational" considerations to override educational purposes. We do it in the schedules we create, the grade groups we assemble, and the way we configure our classrooms. At IPS, we now have single age (but multi-ability) grade groups working within an academic schedule of 45-minute teaching blocks that keep everyone moving at a frantic pace. While this makes a certain amount of sense in terms of staffing efficiencies and hours of instruction requirements, it is not clear that it represented the best conditions in which to educate our students.

The good news is that contemporary schools are now getting more intelligent and more intentional about the design and use of learning spaces. We know that different space configurations encourage (or discourage) different kinds of learning experiences. Seminar tables (or round circles on the floor) offer a good venue for group discussions. Individual cubicles, perhaps with headphones, are a good place for independent study. Open spaces that offer access to large, shared computer monitors can be a good place to collaborate. We know as well that some students will thrive in noise and collective chaos, while others will need solitude and quiet. We have learned, moreover, that the traditional classrooms cannot, by themselves, carry the weight of a rich and meaningful education.

This new understanding is finding its way to schools and classrooms across the land. Some schools have introduced Harkness tables (special seminar tables) as the physical expression of a philosophical commitment to encouraging real discussion amongst students and staff. Additionally, contemporary school designers are now creating more open and variable workspaces that are thought to be better suited to individual and group learning. School libraries are no longer libraries; they are now "learning commons" that combine resource stations with collaborative learning spaces. Classrooms are no longer classrooms; they are meeting pods with movable furniture and glass walls that encourage flexibility and transparency. There is an emerging desire to ensure that space reflects purpose—that form should follow function. This is all to the good. In terms of effecting positive educational change, it is also one of the easiest places to start.

TIME

To conclude this section, let me use a consideration of how time is managed within contemporary middle and high schools as a way to illuminate the structural (architectural) heart of our current system. Here is a list of operational presuppositions that most high school administrators have to deal with:

- Students need to take 6-8 full courses per year.
- Each course (currently) requires about 100 hours of classroom time over the course of an academic year.
- These courses are arranged in grade cohorts wherein students take courses with colleagues of their own age.
- Although students take courses in age-based cohorts, they have some variation in course choices, particularly in high school.
- Each course section (i.e., class) is expected to have, on average, no less than 12 and no more than 30 students.
- Each middle or high school teacher is responsible for all that is involved in teaching 5-6 courses per academic year.
- There are a finite number of teachers (with requisite background qualifications) who can be used to teach courses.
- An academic year runs from 35-45 weeks.
- A school day spans between 5.5 and 6.5 hours, with between 4.5 and 5.5 of that being available for instructional time.
- Students are expected to attend every academic day over the course of a regular academic year (i.e., September to June).
- There are a finite number of instructional spaces that are available in which to hold classes.

The logistical problem that necessarily follows from these presuppositions amounts to figuring out how best to match up a set number of students with a set number of teachers within a defined time so that the students get the "program" they need, and the teachers are used to maximum allowable capacity.

The challenge, therefore, is to create the mother of all timetables. Within the context of the parameters that have been given, the solutions that have emerged have frankly been masterful. Using subtle variations of class lengths and different daily rotation schedules and employing highly sophisticated timetabling programs (particularly in the larger schools), educational administrators have been able to coordinate the academic programs and job assignments of hundreds, even thousands, of students and staff.

But what if it did not have to be this way? What happens when we start to question some of the basic operational assumptions that go into the construction of these kinds of timetables? What if we could figure out a completely different educational architecture that makes these kinds of schedules unnecessary?

Do we always need, for example, roughly 100 hours of instructional time, in a given instructional space, to complete a "course?" Are there parts of these courses that some students can do faster? What allowances should we make for those students who work at a different pace? Come to think of it, does it always make sense to speak in terms of discrete courses? Are there some elements that require longer-term attention over multiple years to be truly educative?

The idea that courses need to be completed in a requisite number of hours goes back to the creation of the "Carnegie Unit" in the late 19th and early 20th centuries. Developed in part to standardize retirement pensions for university professors, the original Carnegie Unit was defined as 120 hours of contact time with an instructor, or 7,200 minutes over an academic year.

Course completion was therefore understood and defined in terms of seat time, not the quality of learning that occurred. In 1993, Ernest L. Boyer, then president at the Carnegie Foundation for the Advancement of teaching, made a speech in which he declared that the Carnegie unit should be made obsolete. He later went on to write, "I urgently hope we can move beyond the old Carnegie units. I find it disturbing that students can complete the required courses, receive a high school diploma, and still fail to gain a more coherent view of knowledge and a more integrated, authentic view of life."[15]

Once the sanctity of course time is challenged, all sorts of other questions follow suit:

- Is it necessarily the case that students need to complete 6-8 "courses" per year to fulfil the requirements of a "program?" Are there other program elements that students might be exposed to that would enable them to acquire a deeper, richer education?

- Are secondary teachers' jobs best defined in terms of how many courses they teach and how much time they spend in the building?

- Should an academic year span 35-45 weeks? Should students be expected to attend an entire academic year? What happens when they do not?

- Can school days, particularly for older students, start later and extend longer into the evening?

- Can we maximize the use of instructional space in a way that best meets the needs of multiple purposes? Are there other spaces outside of schools that could be effectively used for student learning?

We have arrived at the necessity of constructing very sophisticated timeta-bles because we have accepted the presuppositions that go into our current way of operating. If we change just some of these, we might be able to find some breathing space to introduce different learning and engagement elements that significantly enhance the educational experience of our students.

What is abundantly clear is that all these elements are interrelated; to pull on one thread is to unravel a very complex ball of string. But pull we must because, if we do not, we will simply be stuck on the same hamster wheel, forfeiting the opportunity to create a new, different, and better kind of education for our kids. This is what I mean by having the courage to take an architectural approach to educational change.

Structure Matters

Student Assessment & Reporting

Perhaps the most challenging philosophical and structural element we need to re-examine in contemporary education is our approach to student assessment. This is going to be a difficult chapter because much of what I have to say is counterintuitive to that which we understand and are used to. Some of it, in fact, amounts to educational heresy. I have decided to include it in this collection, nonetheless, because I think it strikes to the heart of how we need to change the very way we think about grade school education. The challenge here is that we are so completely habituated to past practice when it comes to student assessment that we can't even see what the problem is.

Here is an analogy to get us started:

Imagine that you are in the very early stages of a romantic relationship with someone. Let's say that you go out for dinner and then, perhaps, dancing. And then, let's say that at the end of the evening, just when you are dropping your partner off at the door, you take it upon yourself to give that person an itemized report of how you think the evening went. You may have created a mini-rubric that includes categories in clothing selection, personal hygiene, choice of food, dinner conversation, ability to dance, and sense of humour. You show your partner how all the individual scores add up to a collective assessment of, for example, 8/10 on your evening out. You assure them that you have used this same system on many other dates, so their ranking is a reliable comparative measure of how they stack up against others.

I think the way we handle assessment in schools is just as awkward, inappropriate, and irrelevant to the project of educating students as the approach that this hapless suitor has taken in the pursuit of a romantic relationship. Just as the suitor has significantly misunderstood the very point and nature of romantic engagement, so too have parents and educators unwittingly endorsed an approach to assessment that fundamentally misunderstands and distorts the point of education.

Let me give you an example to explain what I mean by this. Imagine that we want to introduce students to the world of poetry as a human accomplishment that is worthy of our attention, and perhaps even of a lifelong interest. At base, we want our students to understand what poets are trying to do (use language in as precise a manner as possible to convey human experience) and to appreciate how poetry is different than other practices (such as prose, biography, and history) in this regard. To make this introduction we are likely going to give students examples of poems to examine, point out a few techniques that are employed, and (hopefully) have them write some poems of their own.

But how do we then typically assess a student's "understanding" of poetry? *By focusing on the least important, most peripheral (but most easily measurable) elements of the practice.* English teachers the world over make students memorize the definitions of metaphor, simile, allusion, onomatopoeia, etc. and then happily grade them on their understanding of poetry on the basis of being able to properly identify these techniques in use. We do this because it is much easier to get an "objective" measure of student "understanding" by creating right/wrong questions on a test that will yield a definitive quantitative result (3/10, 6/10, 10/10, etc.). What we have done, in effect, is *narrow, fragment, and trivialize*[1] poetry in a way that reduces it to a mechanical deployment of techniques that doesn't even come close to what poetry is all about.

As it is with poetry, so is it with so many other things in school. The beauty of mathematics gets reduced to formula that need to be memorized[2]; history becomes little more than a series of dates to regurgitate; science is encapsulated as a list of components to be identified on a cell diagram; French is diluted into the successful recital of verb conjugations; and expressing important ideas on paper never gets above or beyond the matter of following a preset essay form. Most of us, depressingly, are all too familiar with this version of what was meant to pass for our introduction to the world of ideas.

Why do we do this? Why do we create these elaborate assessment rubrics to generate a rank-ordered characterization of a student's apparent understanding or ability? And why do so many of our assessment practices have the effect of narrowing, fragmenting, and trivializing the ideas and experiences we want to introduce our students to? Because, at the end of the day, teachers need to come up with a comparative measure of student achievement that they can confidently put in a report card.

Teachers in schools constantly struggle with two separate imperatives when it comes to student assessment. On one hand, in the context of their teaching, they want to find out what students know and what they can do in order to give them substantive feedback so that they might extend their learning. This is known as **formative assessment**; it is meant to happen "along the way" as an aid to both the student and teacher in the pursuit of enhanced understanding or ability. Some examples of formative exchanges include the following:

- diagnostic assessments for the purpose of identifying a student's current level of understanding or ability
- immediate right/wrong feedback (via online platforms or teacher-designed quizzes) of relevant baseline literacy elements

- teacher-designed questions (predetermined and/or in the moment) directed at students in the context of one-to-one meetings or group discussions (with substantive commentary and feedback to follow)
- substantive commentary and feedback on, for example:
  - the structure, coherence, clarity, and veracity of a student's written work
  - the quality of analysis exhibited by a student in the context of some activity or investigation
  - teacher-designed (or student-designed) assignments or projects

On the other hand, teachers are also ever mindful of their obligation to produce report cards which must contain endpoint descriptions—**summative assessments**—of a student's apparent level of achievement. Here is what this process looks like for those of us who work in classrooms:

We are expected to "cover" a curriculum, which means we must introduce and expose students to a range of content and skills that are usually specified by things like "prescribed learning outcomes" (Canada) or "common core" requirements (USA).

In order to do this, we create a mixed set of learning experiences—sometimes baseline literacy acquisition, sometimes exploratory projects—that are designed with the prescribed learning outcomes or common core requirements in mind.

Along the way, we make sure we give students periodic tests to measure their (apparent) understanding of the subject matter under study. We also give them assignments that will be evaluated according to criteria that, in some way, are meant to link back to the prescribed learning outcomes or common core requirements.

Importantly, we make sure we record and retain the evaluative results of all our tests and assignments.

At the end of a designated term, we then compile all of these "marks" to-gether. Sometimes, we give different weight to different elements. Short quizzes, for example, might be weighted at 20% of one's total grade, while exams, essays, or special assignments might be given more weight (often involving considerable arithmetic convolutions).

We then create a "report card" to present our evaluative findings. This usu-ally includes a ranked indication of a student's (apparent) ability or under-standing of the subject matter expressed either in words (excellent, very good, good, satisfactory, adequate, or poor), or as a percentage (90%, 76%, 58%, 40%), or a letter grade (A, B+, C, D, F), or as designation on the Interna-tional Baccalaureate 1-7 scale. Report cards sometimes also make reference to a student's strengths and challenges and almost always include some sort of an evaluation of a student's "work habits."

It is important here to keep in mind, again, the distinction between two dif-ferent aims, or motives, of student assessment. It is one thing to invite a student to participate in a series of learning experiences, all the while giving them the resources and constructive feedback to increase their ability and/or understanding within a particular domain. It is quite another thing to use these educative interactions to produce a rank-ordered description of a student's (apparent) level of "achievement."

It may be asked, "So what, exactly, is the problem here?" It might seem intu-itively obvious that we use certain (formative) assessment practices to try to figure out what students know and can do (so we can further extend their learning), and then later give a (summative) account of what they have ap-parently learned. And doesn't it make sense, in the latter case, that we ren-der student achievement in terms of something like rank-order percentages or grades?

The problem is that the summative characterization of student achievement, as expressed in terms of rank-ordered grades, actually dominates and shapes the entire assessment environment of contemporary schools. In so doing, it threatens the quality and integrity of the educative project in at least four different ways.

First, as already alluded to, an assessment system that is ultimately aimed at generating a rank-ordered description of student achievement will almost necessarily tend toward instructional practices that narrow, fragment, and trivialize the subject matter under study. Consider, again, the poetry example.

Second, assessment systems that claim to offer a definitive (rank-order) characterization of a student's level of "achievement" within a particular domain are plagued with the problem of what is called construct validity—that is, the extent to which a particular assessment result accurately represents a student's *true* knowledge, understanding, or ability in a particular area. Even though some students might present well on a report card, this does not necessarily mean they are, in fact, capable or conversant in a subject area. It is one thing to become successful at writing school science tests; it is quite another to think like a scientist. The problem is that report cards rarely offer a reliable measure of what they appear to be reporting on.

Third, it is frequently the case that assessment systems aimed at generating a rank-ordered description of student achievement will invariably leave out certain elements—sometimes even the most important elements—of a field of study. This has been a long-standing issue in education. In a paper entitled "Impact of Large Scale Testing on the Instructional Activity of Science Teachers", educational researcher Marvin Wideen and his colleagues observed that one of the implications of large-scale testing (in order to generate rank-ordered descriptions of student achievement) was that science teachers in the study "now teach fewer labs and lecture more" and "now must concentrate on objectives and reduce the number of side issues students are able to explore".[3]

In the same study, Wideen and his colleagues were also able to capture a related change in instructional tone and focus from grade eight to grade twelve as the imperative to identify and differentiate different levels of student understanding and ability necessarily increased.

We saw a narrowing of the instructional pattern from grade eight to twelve. As observers, it appeared to us that the most vibrant classes took place at the grade 8 and 10 levels. Grade 12 classes, on the other hand, were marked with a palpable desire to come to grips with the material presented. A sense of fun and enjoyment seemed lacking here. This was work and made to seem so. We sensed a strong need to process a great deal of material very quickly. The single mindedness of the enterprise was underscored by the impatience demonstrated by these students when the teacher withheld answers or ventured into territory that would not appear on the examinations. They had no time for anything extraneous.[4]

This impatience and single mindedness on the part of senior students carries on to this day. I have a good friend who taught grade 11 and 12 courses for several years in a high-end independent school. He has two stories that chill me to the bone.

In the course of a grade 11 Theory of Knowledge seminar class, he made a point of posing provocative questions in an attempt to have his students grapple with the various concepts they had been studying. While some of his student undoubtedly enjoyed his repartee—he is a very intelligent and engaging teacher—one student expressed his frustration (and his perception of the reality of his situation) by saying, "Mr. X, we just need you to give us the correct answer so we can get the grade we need to get into the university that our parents want us to get into."

In another instance, my friend had counseled his students that it was likely counterproductive for them to cram for their final exams. (He taught at an International Baccalaureate school.) Despite his advice, many of his students showed up early on the morning of their exam day to participate in a frenzied last-minute review. When he asked them why they were doing this, they replied that it would be worth it if they could score just one more point on their test. When he pointed out that they would probably quickly forget whatever it was that they crammed into their heads, they immediately replied, "We don't care."

The fourth problem with an assessment system that is aimed at generating a rank-ordered description of student achievement is that it necessarily captures a very narrow band of student dispositions, competence, understanding, and ability. We all know what it takes to be academically successful at school, particularly in the senior years:

- listen attentively in class
- take good notes
- "study hard" (review material on a consistent basis)
- get tutorial help when needed
- write and speak clearly
- pay close attention to instructions and follow them meticulously
- gain a sense of what your teacher wants (in structure, content, and form) and do that
- hand assignments in on time
- ask insightful questions
- take care in presenting your work
- work well with others

If a student does all these things, they will be appreciated in class and do well on tests and assignments. There are, in other words, certain repertoires that need to be performed—certain ways of being—that will result in better evaluations.

Consider, however, the difference between the so-called "good" and "bad" (or "struggling") students in the context of most contemporary high schools. The "good" students do all of the things on the list. They know that academic success is not rocket science: it is a matter of understanding the game and doing what needs to be done.

The so-called "bad" (or "struggling") students live in a completely different world:

- They don't "listen in class" because they can't, in fact, hear; or because they can't process oral information quickly; or because they need to render ideas in visual form before they understand them. (They make jokes or socialize with their friends because if they can't be successful as students, they need to be successful at something else.)

- They are incapable of "taking good notes" because they do not know what that would look like, given the particular way they learn, and they are, in any case, stunned and baffled by the classroom environment.

- They are decidedly disinclined to "review material on a consistent basis" because they have not been given a credible enough reason why it should deserve their immediate attention, or because they are so frustrated by their apparent inability to understand the subject matter they would prefer not to prolong the agony.

- They do not "get tutorial help when needed" because, in their eyes, this only draws attention to their perceived inabilities; or because the tutorial help they have been given has been inefficient; or because the tutorial appointments conflict with their sports or dance activities.

- They can't "write clearly" because they haven't been taught to think clearly; or because they haven't been given the time to figure out what they want to say; or because no one has shown them how to organize their thoughts (let alone incorporate other people's ideas into their own position). They can't "speak clearly" because they are too shy, sensitive, anxious, or nervous to do so in public; or because they have not been required, out of school, to present ideas in a coherent form; or because they have an elliptical way of eventually arriving at a conclusion by way of a stream-of-consciousness examination of ideas, and there is no time for that in a classroom.

- They have a hard time "paying close attention to instructions and following them meticulously" because they have lost the instructions and do not know how to retrieve them digitally; or because they become so excited about their own interpretation of an assignment that their enthusiasm causes them to overlook what is actually being asked for; or because they find themselves overwhelmed by the assignment (because they do not know how to translate the instructions into action); or because they do not think the assignment is worth doing in the first place.

- They likewise have difficulty "gaining a sense of what their teachers want and then doing that" because they are incapable of picking up on the social cues that most adults use to indicate when something is important; or because they do not care what a particular teacher wants because that teacher has not created a relationship of trust and respect with them.

- They rarely "hand things in on time" because they haven't been shown how to manage their time and priorities; or because they do not regard their school assignments as priorities relative to the other things they do; or because other conditions (such as depression or anxiety) or other situations (troubles at home) are overtaking their lives.

- They are unable to "ask insightful questions" in class because they are incapable of following the thread of oral conversation that is unfolding; or because they are justifiably afraid of asking the wrong question because they have seen questions met with ridicule before; or because they haven't been shown the value of asking questions and given the license and encouragement to do so; or because they have not seen the connection between their own lives and the subject matter under study.

- They typically do not "take care in presenting their work" because they are dyslexic so they are incapable of detecting most spelling and grammar mistakes (and they do not have the resources or support to proofread their work); or because they have an external passion (competitive gymnastics, dance, or skiing) which makes it difficult for them to find time to put the finishing touches on their work; or because they do not think this particular assignment is worthy of their best effort.

- And finally, these "bad" (or struggling) students typically do not "work well with others" because the others they are supposed to work well with are so completely different from themselves.

The problem is that in having built an assessment environment that celebrates the "good" student and disenfranchises the "bad," we have summarily failed to capture and encourage the potential capacity of a significant portion of our student population. And worse, in some cases we have contributed to the creation of an unwarranted negative self-image in these so-called "bad" students that can follow them for the rest of their lives. This is not only immoral; it is a colossal waste of the human spirit.[5]

A DIFFERENT WAY OF THINKING

As with most challenges in education, the heart of the problem centers on the question of fundamental purpose—i.e., why before how. If we think that the core purpose of a grade school education is to produce a rank-ordered description of student "achievement" (as defined within a school context), our current assessment practices are perfectly aligned with that aim. If, however, we think that the core purpose of grade school education might be something deeper and richer than that—*to equip and inspire stu-*

dents to cultivate their humanity—we need a different way to approach student assessment in the context of that aim.

To cut right to the chase, the problem is not our use of formative assessment. Insofar as teachers are committed to enhancing student learning, it is completely appropriate for them to use all kinds of measures to figure out what kids apparently know or can do.[6] As mentioned, these might include diagnostic tests, right/wrong assessments on baseline literacy elements, and substantive teacher feedback on assignments. All of these can and should be employed in the service helping students extend their learning.

The real challenge is coming up with a different approach to *summative assessments*—those endpoint descriptions of what students have accomplished over the course of their grade school education. In doing this, we need to be mindful of how easy it is for the "tail to wag the dog", in other words, for the endpoint assessment to shape and potentially distort the day-to-day practice. Reducing poetry to answering multiple choice questions on the definitions of metaphors and similes is a good example of this. If we can create endpoint descriptions that are more nuanced and ambitious, however, we can create an assessment environment that supports, rather than sabotages, our deeper purposes.

The short story answer here is that we need to shift away from traditional report cards that offer rank-order descriptions of student achievement within different subject areas and move toward a more sophisticated use of something like portfolios and individual learner profiles. We need to create a more multilayered and fine-grained record of what students have actually done, what they are interested in, and what attributes they demonstrably possess. And we need to do this in a way that captures and reveals a broader range of understanding and ability than is typically embedded within a standard report card.

But I imagine something different than a standard portfolio that simply highlights the student's best work. I imagine something more along the lines of a comprehensive "learner profile" that includes not only a detailed list of what exactly the student has done but also an indication of their interests and their demonstrable strengths as a person.

What might this look like? It might begin with a *summary page* something along the lines of the example sketched out on the next two pages.

LEARNER PROFILE
Urban Pacific Collegiate
STUDENT: Eliza McPherson   **DATE:** June, 2020

Workshops Attended and Completed
- Time Management and Executive Functioning
- How to Read a Book
- Incorporating External Content Into Research Papers
- Working in Collaborative Groups
- Design Thinking
- Introduction to Practical Reasoning *etc.*

Baseline Literacy Elements Acquired to a Mastery Level
- Basic Sentence Structure
- Reading Comprehension (to Level 4)
- Mathematical Operations (to Level 6)
- Distinguishing Types of Claims in Arguments
- Eight Common Fallacies *etc.*

Foundation Courses Completed (Pass/Fail)
- A Brief History of Civilization
- On the Shoulders of Giants: A Survey of Human Science
- Human Communication: Music, Art, and Literature

Independent Courses Completed (Instructor Certified)
- Investigations in Biological Systems
- Big History[7]
- How to Make an App
- Watercolour painting *etc.*

Teacher-Assigned Projects
- Mystery of the Great Pyramid [History, Mathematics, Science] [Collaborative]
- Scientist Profile: Madame Currie [Science; History] [Individual]
- Thinker Profile: Hildegaard of Bingen [Philosophy; History] [Individual]
- Math Profile: The Fibonnaci Sequence [Math; History] [Individual]
- Creative Arts Profile: Jackson Pollack *etc.*

Self-Designed Projects (Self-Report and Profile Tags)
- Explorations of a Single Cell [Biological Science]
- Developing an App to Understand Cell Biology [Graphic Design; Technology; Science]
- Masterworks: Contemporary Fashion Design *etc.*

External Credentials
- St. John's Ambulance First Aid
- Duke of Edinburgh (Silver)
- Computer Graphics for Gaming (Level 1)
- Carpentry Apprentice (Level 1)

Interests and Points of Engagement
- Biology
- Graphic Design for Digital interfaces
- History (particularly women's history)

Demonstrable Personal Attributes
- Persistence & Tenacity [links to specific examples]
- Attention to Detail [links to specific examples]
- Able to learn from others and incorporate external ideas into her own thinking [links to specific examples]

The summary above is a partial representation of the kind of thing that might be produced at the conclusion of the senior (grade 12) year of study. While these kinds of summaries could, in fact, be produced at any time, this "graduating" summary would focus particularly on those elements completed in the senior years.

There are a couple of features of this kind of a "learner profile" that are worthy of note. The first is that the top three sections refer to the kinds of elements that might be required of all students, such as learning skills workshops, mastery of certain baseline literacy requirements, and exposure to a few foundational survey courses (however configured) that attempt to help students connect the dots between the multitudinous stories of human achievement and folly. These represent, perhaps, the minimal requirements of engaged citizenship.

The remaining six sections are explicitly designed to provide a more direct and substantive account of the differentiated strengths, interests, and attributes of individual learners. The Independent Courses completed will be chosen by the student (in conjunction with a program advisor) based on the student's individual strengths and interests and their post-graduate aspirations. (Some of these courses might be taken via online or third-party institutions.[8]) Even the teacher-directed projects (that, in many cases, would be linked to the courses) will admit of differentiation in that there will always be options to select within a given domain. The self-designed projects—progressively more ambitious versions of the IPS Masterworks—will be the best indicators of a student's individual strengths and interests. The External Credentials Earned and the declared Interests and Demonstrable Attributes are meant to fill out and further establish the unique learner profile of each particular student.

A second important feature of this "learner profile" is its focus on mastery-level accomplishment and pass/fail assessments over rank-order descriptions of student achievement. There are a multitude of baseline literacy elements and basic skills that can and should be taught to all students to a mastery level. (As the profile implies, however, these elements should make up a limited part of a student's total program.) The challenge and the commitment is to make sure we create the right structure and the right student support systems to make sure this happens for each and every student.

Similarly, we need to design our courses—whatever they happen to be—in a way that the minimum requirements for a "pass" are clearly understood, and then leave it at that. These minimum requirements *might* include some combination of the following:

- designated minimum hours of attendance
- successful completion of baseline comprehension elements
- submission of a requisite number of genuine questions
- participation in class discussions or online forums
- completion of a designated number of experiments

- submission to the class of a required number of related external references or articles
- successful completion of a requisite number of papers or projects

The point is, once the student has completed the stipulated requirements, they have passed the course. It will not be a matter of getting an "A" or a "72%"; it will instead be a matter of engaging in the course to the level required.

The best way to reveal a student's unique strengths, interests and abilities is by way of what they actually do—the kinds of independent courses they complete, the external credentials they earn, the projects they take on, and the way they conduct themselves throughout the year. The proof is in the pudding. The proposition here is that it is these sorts of things—more than any attenuated approximation of student "achievement" embedded in a grade—that best capture the true capacity and potential of individual students.

Not incidentally, a third notable feature of this summary page is the inclusion of a student's declared "Interests" and/or points of engagement. This is not something we usually include in summative assessments because, unfortunately, it is not something we pay much attention to in schools. We tell students what courses they need to take and what specific assignments they need to complete in order to make it through the system. I suspect that one of the reasons there is so little individual student agency in schools is that assessment is very much an external proposition. By including a personal declaration of interests in this resume—and, indeed, by having the senior years, in particular, emphasize the discovery and development of individual strengths and passions—we create an environment where what goes on in schools actually matters to students.

A final, more operational, feature of this "learner resume" is that the summary page would be constructed in a way to provide links back to foundational data as a way to support abbreviated claims being made in the summary document, particularly with regard to strengths, interests, and attributes as follows:

- The summary page might indicate an interest and ability in biology. How is this supported? Click onto the biology courses completed, the field work done over spring break, and perhaps most importantly, the individual research on cell division in the grade 11 project that was endorsed by an external scientist in the field.

- The summary page might indicate that the student is a "self-starter" who "takes initiative." How is this supported? Click onto the three clubs the student started in high school and the app she developed for her senior Masterworks project in grade 12.

I wrote earlier of presenting the "short story" version of this different approach to summative assessment. A more detailed description of how we might proceed would likely involve the creation of a two-part mechanism: a) a large *repository* of student accomplishments and experiences, and b) a resultant *profile* that is drawn out of that repository. The "summary page" is actually the profile that it is drawn out of the complete "portfolio" (or repository) of student experience. The repository could have built into it certain digital tags to identify content areas (math, science, history, etc.) and certain attributes, such as persistence, attention to detail, etc. (In the summary page above, I have included examples of some possible tags via the descriptors in box brackets.) It could also have, built into it, credibility and endorsement tags, but that is indeed a longer story. The most important point, for the time being, is that we need to move forward toward a more multi-layered and fine-grained mechanism that will offer a reliable and credible account of what an individual has actually done and where their interests, abilities, and aspirations actually lie.

Two objections will immediately come to the foreground, the first of which is solvable, and the second of which actually represents an invitation for education to move into the 21st century.

The first objection has to do with privacy of personal data. In any scheme that proposes repositories of student data that would then be used to generate individual profiles, the issue of privacy is bound to come up. When this book was being written, the Facebook breach (via Cambridge Analytica) was much in the news.[9] What readers might not know is that Edmodo, a popular digital-learning platform, had also been hacked, resulting in—as education commentator Benjamin Herold reported—"the personal information of an estimated 77 million users being put up for sale on an unregulated part of the internet."[10]

While these developments are indeed worrying, there are nonetheless ways to mitigate against such eventualities. The Future Ready Schools consortium, for example, has Data and Privacy protocols as one of its essential "gears" in its Future Ready Framework. One of its policy provisions is that "District data will not be made available or sold for marketing purposes."[11] It is likely that most, if not all, educational authorities will follow suit. While some commentators have suggested that the digital terrain may have resembled something akin to the wild west in the past, it is unlikely to continue to do so in the future.[12]

The second question that will undoubtedly arise is how college and university admissions officers will be able to make sense of everything submitted in a student profile. The worry is that they will just be too difficult to interpret.[13] Presumably the perceived core advantage of percentage scores and grade-point averages is that, even though they might be regarded as an imperfect indicator of student interest and ability, they nonetheless provide specific cut-off criteria for oversubscribed admissions.

The truth of the matter, however, is that more and more colleges and universities are already starting to use a broader range of indicators to make their admissions decisions. In 2016, the Coalition for Access, Affordability, and Success[14] introduced a new portfolio-based application platform that is accepted by over 120 universities in the United States, including Harvard, Yale, and Princeton. The platform includes a special "Locker" feature that encourages students from grade nine onward to submit examples of their best work as part of a four-year pre-planning exercise aimed at college attendance. University admissions proponents of the platform like having the flexibility to select different elements from the student portfolio to add some texture to their selection process.

While all of this is promising, I look forward to the day when colleges and universities will have the capacity to do away with grade-point averages altogether—the capacity, that is, to see students for who they really are. If they do this, they will get better match-ups for their programs, and they will contribute to an educational transformation that finally enables grade schools to focus on what matters most.

This proposed shift in assessment toward repositories and profiles is really an invitation to all students—but to senior students, in particular—to take more ownership over their own learning and indeed their own definition of who they are.

It is also meant to underline a shift in the way we understand the purpose of grade-school education. Our assessment mechanisms should not be engineered to identify, in Thorndike's language, the "winners and losers." They should instead be engineered to enable students to discover and develop their unique interests, abilities, and aspirations.

It is true that some people are better at performing the repertoires required at school and may even be cognitively faster than others at seeing connections and relationships between things. It is also obvious that we can't be outstanding or even proficient in all things. I will never be a brilliant mathematician. But all of this is irrelevant to the task of giving all students an education that will enable and encourage each one of them to express the very best of who they are. Each one of us has the capacity to be good at something. The assessment mechanisms we use in grade school should be aimed at finding out what that something is.

Those senior educators that I spoke about in the Preface who dreamed of a different way to approach student assessment were rightfully worried that, in the absence of a compelling alternative, "the parents would never go for it." Here is that compelling alternative: an approach to student assessment that actively seeks out, develops, and recognizes the distinctive interests and abilities of our children. This is not a winner take all system; it is instead an architecture that encourages and celebrates the contributions and unique gifts of each and every person. It is the kind of assessment approach that best realizes the goal of equipping and inspiring students to cultivate their humanity.

Structure Matters

Educational Finance

Another difficult structural matter to confront is the whole issue of educational finance. Where do we get the money to do the things we need to do to re-engineer our schools? How best do we deploy our financial resources? The topic here is vast and frankly warrants another book. The most I can offer, at present, are a few initial observations.

The first of these is that if we are interested in creating impactful education for all students, and if we consider that over 90% of students attend public schools, we need to find a way to create remarkable schools within the manageable parameters of public funding. Private and independent schools will make their own way—usually, but not exclusively—by way of significant tuition fees. If we are looking for a more profound social transformation, however, this can only come through a sufficiently revitalized public education system.

Canada currently spends about $12,000 (CND) per student each year on public education, when capital and operating costs are taken together.[1] America spends about $12,000 (USD) per year, although only 70% of total educational expenditures in the USA (i.e., $8,500)[2] come from public funding. The rest comes from parents and private sources. If the goal is to at least match current *public* expenditures, the challenge is to operate schools in Canada and the USA with approximately $12,000 (CAD) and $8,500 (USD)[3] per year, respectively, of government funding.

This will be difficult, but not impossible. Some private schools in the USA and independent schools in Canada[4] are already operating at below this level. These are typically alternate or religious schools that operate on bare subsistence budgets.

There is also a separate category of *publicly-funded* schools—called charter schools—that are independently run, charge no tuition fees, and receive more or less the same funding as the public schools[5]. While the debate for and against these independently-run charter schools is complex and highly political[6], the fact that they operate primarily on public funding[7] is noteworthy.

The caution regarding both private and charter school alternatives, however, is that quality is sometimes compromised to cost, and the people working in these schools are not always appropriately paid for what they contribute. The financial challenge for any new model of public education is to ensure the best possible program for students, while at the same time sustaining—and in fact celebrating—the professionalism of educational providers.

A LITTLE BIT MORE AND CERTAINLY NOT LESS

Defenders of public education like to propose that the solution to improved schooling is simple: it is merely a matter of governments "realigning their priorities" to provide more money for education. These folks are sometimes fond of quoting Robert Fulghum who said, "It will be a great day when our schools have all the money they need, and our air force has to have a bake-sale to buy a bomber." Although I agree that part of the solution must include a renewed commitment to public education on the part of governments, I don't think that this is going to be the complete answer.

Educational funding in Canada and the USA is usually the second highest expenditure in most jurisdictions, exceeded only by health care and/or public welfare. While government budgets typically amount to billions of dollars, they are nonetheless not infinite. When advocates talk of shifting priorities, what other services do they imagine being cut? If we imagine that the solution will be for "the government" to significantly increase taxes, we need to remember who foots the bill for that. Going forward, I think that—with some notable exceptions[8]—we should assume and expect incrementally increased public funding for grade school education but without large leaps.

On the other hand, I think it is foolish to imagine that we can create remarkable schools with any *less* money than current public expenditures. Advocates of charter schools sometimes try to make this case by claiming that their schools can deliver "bigger bang for the educational buck" by eliminating "layers of expensive (and meddlesome) bureaucracy" and providing "real accountability for results[9]. This is simplistic, and it takes us in precisely the wrong direction when it comes to the issue of educational funding. Similarly, proponents of alternative education schemes sometimes like to imply that teacher salaries can be reduced by, for example, shifting more educational delivery to software platforms. I think this is a false assumption that is going to impede widespread adoption of new initiatives within the public system as a whole. The place to start is to assume that funding for salaries will remain the same—or will be increased where necessary—and go from there. Education is a public good; however configured, it deserves and requires as much financial support as we can provide.

GETTING CREATIVE

In the same way that we need to be prepared to change the way we think about education, so too must we be prepared to change the way we think about certain elements of educational finance.

Notwithstanding the point about maintaining, or improving, educator salaries, it will likely be the case that the *job descriptions* of educational providers will need to change. If the traditional role of teachers becomes separated out into more manageable parts—i.e., with a view to enabling the right person to end up with the right job—then the funding structure for particular job responsibilities will change as well.

It might also be the case that different delivery configurations—regarding group size and composition, timetabling, and use of instructional space—will require different levels of funding. What might be optimum for elementary or middle school will likely be different than what works best for secondary education. The point is to do the analysis in a way that *begins with* the best configuration for each division and then build the relevant financial architecture to sustain it.

Finally, the *intelligent* use of educational technology is also going to play a part in enabling us to build a sustainable financial structure to underpin remarkable schools. While it is clear that there is a place for online learning platforms to address some elements of a student's overall education, we need to be careful that we do not let the pursuit of "cost efficiencies" cheapen and trivialize the learning process. As intimated in the previous chapter, I suspect that one of the best uses of technology will be the creation of sophisticated student management systems that enable students and program mentors to direct and document the specific achievements and explorations of individual learners.

UNTAPPED RESOURCES?

One final conjecture about educational funding in the future: it may be that the public system will need to do something that independent schools have been doing for years—*ask their constituents and their community for help*. There is no reason why individuals and businesses should not be making significant donations to public education. Just as everyday donors and large-scale philanthropists contribute to all sorts of public institutions like libraries, museums, and art galleries, so too should we cultivate a sensibility that public education, in particular, is more than deserving of our support.

After I left my own independent school, I made a point of making a yearly donation to our local public school, with the proviso that the funds be spent "at the discretion of the principal." Although the amount wasn't significant, the intent was. I wanted to underline my commitment to public education, and I also wanted to make sure the principal was in the driver's seat as to how the funds would be spent. While my donation was relatively small, what would happen if the thousands and thousands of families associated with public schools were to do the same thing?

I am not advocating here a new funding model whereby these donations become an essential component of the overall financial structure. Our tax system remains the most stable, equitable, and appropriate way to support education. I am suggesting, however, that this kind of micro-funding might go a long way to enable site-based principals to pursue special initiatives that could have a real impact.

I think we sometimes underestimate the importance of inviting people to contribute to a project that is worth doing. At my school, we were able to build a strong sense of community because everyone had some skin in the game. In the case of creating a strong public education system for all, I can't help but think that—given a powerful enough clarion call to significantly improve our schools—there may yet be a groundswell of supporters who might be prepared to take up the challenge. There is only one way to find out.

Possible Futures

Outlier Schools: What Can We Learn From Them?

In what follows, I am going to offer five brief case studies of schools that, in one way or another, developed their own independent answer to what might constitute a great education. It needs to be said at the outset that these schools are all outliers. They all operate in some way independently from their respective public school systems. They have all developed different approaches to the traditional model of education and have attracted families and students to their schools on the basis of their distinctive philosophy. They are all new schools that have been established within the last two decades, and most of them receive external funding to build and maintain parts of their program.[1] I think it will be useful, nonetheless, to see what we can learn from these innovators, educators, and parents who have decided to break the mold and try something different.

HIGH TECH HIGH

Founded in 2000 by a coalition of "San Diego business leaders and educators" to "prepare a diverse range of students for postsecondary education, citizenship, and leadership in the high technology industry"[2], High Tech High has used *project-based learning* as their centerpiece to fundamentally restructure the educational experience of its students. The basic idea is that teachers design compelling projects for students to complete and then present at public "exhibitions." One example offered on their website is a project entitled "Newton's Games," which would have students explore and incorporate some law of physics into an applicable game.[3]

The High Tech High concept includes more than just project-based learning, however. It is, in fact, a fully-articulated alternative vision of education that is grounded in four self-described design principles: *personalization; adult world connection; and common intellectual mission, teacher as designer*. The school correctly points out that these design principles, in turn, "call for structures and practices that schools do not now routinely employ." In addition to the focus on project-based learning, they cite "the small size of the school, the openness of the facilities, the personalization through advisory, the requirement that all students complete internships in the community, and the provision of ample planning time for teacher teams during the work day as being essential to their model."

What started as one high school in 2000, has since grown to an organization of four elementary schools, four middle schools, and six high schools in the San Diego area. These are public charter schools where students are accepted by lottery, with five applicants for every available space. They are extremely thoughtful about their growth model. While they expect each school to adopt its own unique culture, they nonetheless take what they call a "mitochondrial" approach wherein they seed new schools with a principal, teachers, and even students who have already lived and worked in a High Tech High school.[4] Now serving some 5,000 students, the High Tech High model offers a very compelling educational reconfiguration that is likely going to gain even more traction in the future.

SUMMIT SCHOOLS

The Summit Public Schools network is a formidable operation. After giving the original Summit Prep school a significant makeover in 2012, CEO Diana Tavenner and her colleagues went on to open seven other middle and high schools in the San Francisco Bay area and three additional schools in Washington State. In 2015, they offered to share their distinctive educational model for free, and 330 partner schools across the United States have since come on board.[5]

There are three central pillars to the Summit Schools educational framework: *project-based learning focused on cognitive skills; self-paced learning to mastery in content areas; and one-to-one mentoring* to help students set and meet goals. The centerpiece of their model is an online platform that tracks student progress across the entire program. According to freelance education writer Joanna Jacobs,

> *"Students master academic content through personalized learning, choosing from 'playlists' made of such learning tools as Khan Academy videos, BrainPOP animations, guided practice problems, interactive exercises, websites, and texts. They take tests when they feel ready, moving on to new content when they've achieved mastery. A blue line on the student's dashboard shows whether he or she is progressing at the expected rate."[6]*

Jacobs reports that Summit students spend about 80% of their days working on projects, while 20% of their time is devoted to Personalized Learning Time (PLT), "during which students learn academic content, choosing the digital tools they'll use to meet their goals."[7]

In terms of assessment, about 30% of a student's final grade is based on "content knowledge," as determined by achieving mastery—8 out of 10—on multiple choice assessments. "The other 70% comes from some 200 different projects, designed to enhance students' cognitive skills."[8] By "cognitive skills," the Summit Schools folks have in mind "problem-solving, effective communicating, creative thinking, writing and speaking."[9]

Some Summit teachers have become real enthusiasts. Joanne Jacobs describes how Brandy Holton, a Summit teacher, reports that she "used to spend hours every night custom planning lessons for 7th graders at different levels, searching for resources and creating videos."

"It was exhausting," said Holton. Now, with most tools and materials included in the platform, "I'm re-energized. The teacher guilt is gone."[10]

Grade 8 English teacher Kevin Kreller concurs that the Summit schools are a great place to teach. Jacobs quotes him as saying that this has been the "most rewarding teaching" he has ever done, partially because he has more time to give students "real, meaningful feedback" and build relationships.[11]

ALTSCHOOL

Created in 2014 by Founder and CEO Max Ventilla, the AltSchool set out to revolutionize education by creating a personalized learning technology to serve as the centerpiece for an integrated program that would develop the whole child.

Like High Tech High, the AltSchool model includes *interdisciplinary project-based learning* and the importance of exploring community resources (e.g., art galleries, community mentors) to make what they describe as *"real-world connections"* between what students are studying and the world outside the classroom. The truly distinctive element of the Alt Schools, however, is the way that it uses its *proprietary technology to support and promote personalized learning.*

Mr. Ventilla, a successful entrepreneur who has founded and sold several technology companies, was one of the first six people to work on the Google Plus platform. In an introductory video on the Alt Schools site, he tells us that he has "worked continuously to build products and technology that lets people connect with each other and lead fuller lives."[12] He also tells us that his aspiration is to create "an education model that can scale, can improve, the more people participate in it"...[and one that will]..."deliver what we would want for our own kids, and what we would want for our own country and our world." Central to the AltSchool architecture is the continuous use of very sophisticated software to capture each student's individual progress in their own online "Learning Progression."

In a feature article on AltSchool published in the *New Yorker* magazine on March 7, 2016, Rebecca Mead describes AltSchool teacher Christie Seyfert's use of the Learning Progression as follows:

> "Seyfert pulled up the Learning Progression spreadsheet of one of her students, a seventh grader. Grades from kindergarten to eighth grade were denoted on the X axis, and various subject areas on the Y axis. Areas of completed study—sixth-grade math, for example—were indicated by cells filled in with green. Areas the student was still working on—seventh-grade science, for instance—were colored orange. In English, he was working well ahead of his expected grade level.

> "Seyfert could click on each subject area to get more precise information about his progress. The effect was rather like opening an online report from a credit-card company that can show expenditures by category—Shopping, Travel—as well as specific purchases. She could see how many articles the student had read on Newsela, a site that provides Associated Press articles edited for different reading levels. She could click to see the student's scores on the quizzes that accompanied each article, and then go into the article itself to read his annotations and marginal notes."[13]

What is distinctive about the AltSchool's program architecture is the way it seeks to use the big data of infinite educational interactions to provide feedback to teachers and students to continually improve the learning experience. As we will see in the commentary below, this approach brings with it both possibilities and pitfalls.

PACIFIC SCHOOL OF INNOVATION AND INQUIRY (PSII)

In 2013, Jeff Hopkins left his job as superintendent of the Gulf Islands School District in British Columbia to create the Pacific School of Innovation and Inquiry (PSII), a very different grade 9-12 high school in Victoria, British Columbia. He was much taken by the Russian psychologist Lev Vygotsky's notion of "the zone of proximal development"—i.e., the idea that there is a sweet spot in learning directly in between the things you already know and the things that are too far past your ability to comprehend. It is that sweet spot that offers the greatest potential for new learning. The PSII website points out, importantly, that this zone is different for each person, a basic fact that most contemporary schools are not equipped to deal with.[14]

In describing their underlying philosophy, the PSII website makes a distinction between what they call the "emergent curriculum" and the "common curriculum." The idea of the emergent curriculum is that "what needs/wants to be learned emerges through the teaching and learning relationship and is informed by earlier learning." The common curriculum refers to those learning goals "that are universal, but which can still be addressed through the individual lens created by and for each learner." At PSII about 85% of the time is devoted to the emergent curriculum—i.e., through the pursuit of individualized investigations—while only 15% of the time is taken up by the common curriculum.[15]

In order to underline how PSII is different than traditional high schools, their website also offers a useful comparative table:[16]

	Most High Schools	PSII

Subjects, Courses and Classes	Subjects are segregated into separate courses/classes where BC curriculum is covered.	Subjects are integrated; the BC curriculum is **un**covered in interdisciplinary combinations
Level of Personalization	Courses are pre-designed for a batch of 20 to 30 students with some post-design differentiation after the fact based on student need/interest in some cases	Personal learning paths are co-created by learners and teachers. Intersection points and emerging needs/goals inform what is done individually and what is done in groups
Curriculum Design	Curriculum is built on "behavioural outcomes" where every student is asked to demonstrate the same learning behaviour. Some competencies are also referenced but are lower on the hierarchy than the outcomes.	Curriculum is built on personal curiosity through a close learner-teacher relationship, with room for occasional "nudges" by the teacher in to areas of learning the learner may not have thought of alone. Learning is based on valued human attributes, then competencies, then personal and universal learning goals.
How Learners are Grouped	Students are typically grouped by age/grade level. Classes are organized ahead of time and groupings do not change for a semester of a whole year.	Learners are grouped when it makes sense in whatever configuration makes sense. Sometimes by interest, sometimes by similarity, sometimes by difference. Groupings are dynamic.
Learning Environment	"Classrooms" are the main units of learning, so school buildings are organized into rooms of 20 to 30 to hold the average batch size. Some rooms are specialized but	Learners are the main units of learning, and so the school has micro-environments of many different shapes and sizes. Some areas are specialized, but almost everything is flexible.

	many are generic.	
Connection to Greater Community	School tries to offer hypothetical models within the school walls to allow students to demonstrate learning and skill development. Community-based projects are the exception.	Learners are encouraged to develop real projects, based on their own inquiries, and to access the world outside for mentorship, modeling, ideas for future projects, and as a place for them to contribute to society.
Face-to-Face or Virtual?	Most high schools are either face-to-face or are based in a "distributed learning" model where students access learning via technology. Almost all face-to-face is with a teacher alone, and almost all virtual access looks a lot like correspondence courses, only on a computer screen.	PSII learners will be in a hybrid environment by necessity. There is no substitute for face-to-face (at least 90% of what students will experience each day) when human relationships are valued, but because learners could be learning almost anything at any time, virtual experts will often comprise part of the resources learners will access.
Physical Health	Physical education is taught in a gym, with team sports as the main method of providing physical activity. Everyone in a PE class usually does the same thing at the same time, regardless of experience, preference, body type, or health status.	Learners will learn about a holistically healthy lifestyle, including physical health, and will co-create a physical health plan (and assess progress) with a teacher, but will experience it at the Victoria YMCA and other locations that best fit the personal learning goals.

Because the Pacific Academy of Innovation and Inquiry is such a new school, it is perhaps too early to tell whether the idea will catch on. As a working exemplar of at least one clear alternative to the traditional model of schooling, however, it certainly offers us food for thought.[17]

WESTSIDE MINIVERSITY

Graham Baldwin is something of an educational maverick. After serving as Head of School of two prestigious independent schools in British Columbia—one of which he built up from its second year of operation and another he saved from financial disaster—he decided to embark on yet another adventure by transforming the newly-created Westside School in downtown Vancouver, British Columbia. Westside is a K-12 independent school with three separate divisions: the Foundation Years Program (K-4), the Middle Years Program (5-9), and the Miniversity (10-12). While each of these programs is innovative in their own right, it is the grade 10-12 Miniversity[18] that is truly breaking new ground.

Mr. Baldwin had seen first hand the challenges and obstructions that come from running a traditional high school year on a standard linear schedule. He saw that there is no flexibility—no breathing room—in a traditional schedule to enable students to immerse themselves in their studies in a way that would allow for genuine engagement and true understanding. He therefore turned the standard academic schedule on its head by creating an academic year of six instructional (investigative) blocks of 20 days duration, each separated by five-day-intervals to be used for extended work or special symposia. In each 20-day block, a student studies one course only, with teachers correspondingly being responsible for one course at a time.

This single structural move opens up all kinds of possibilities. While the instructional approaches are ever-evolving, what typically happens is that students and teachers begin their day with some sort of a focus lesson followed by instructions and/or invitations about how to proceed independently. Some students will then go off and study on their own, while others might form spontaneous study groups to work through material. Students are directed toward online resources as the teacher sees fit. As mentioned in a prior section on "Student Support," this open scheduling arrangement also allows teachers to give remedial support to students in need. Each teacher, in any case, serves as a mentor for a cohort of 10-12 students.

Because students are not taking 6-8 courses simultaneously, they have the luxury of being able to drill down deeply into whatever they are investigating. Their teachers can also schedule relevant off-site excursions and book in guest speakers to augment and enrich the learning experience. The many testimonials from students indicate that it is a structure, and a learning community, that they appreciate.

COMMENTARY AND CAUTION

While there are differences of emphasis and application in these examples, most of these schools are experimenting with innovations in four key operational domains:

Use of Digital Resources:
- Some reliance on online programs to deliver at least some baseline literacy or core skills requirements, for example using proprietary or open source software like Khan Academy or Duolingo for math and language skills, respectively
- Some digital repository of learning activities or projects—often called a playlist—that student access to work through a teacher-directed and/or self-directed progression of study that is in some way tailored to the student's individual learning needs and/or interests
- Some method of tracking student progress (such as via a "dashboard") with regard to both academic and, in some cases, non-academic pursuits

Instructional Delivery:
- An increasing and concerted interest in using blended learning approaches to appropriately mix teacher-directed and student-directed online learning
- An ever-evolving appreciation of those components of an educational environment that are best handled by face-to-face interactions with teachers and learning support providers (e.g., project development and support, Socratic dialogues, and remedial help)

Program Components:
- A concerted interest in using project-based learning as a significant or even dominant mechanism of student investigation
- A concerted interest in extending the boundaries and resources of education beyond the classroom walls to create so-called "real world" experiences for students. (e.g., excursions, apprenticeships, and external mentors)
- A concerted interest in attempting to address and cultivate qualities of "character," however defined

Structural Changes:
- An increasing appreciation for the way that differential learning spaces can enhance the educational experience for students
- A willingness to attempt different learning configurations other than grade and age specific learning cohorts
- A willingness to explore more flexible learning schedules for both individual learners and group learning cohorts

While these elements, taken together, might offer an enticing template of where grade school education should possibly head in the future, there is at least one preliminary caution we might bear in mind before rushing head-long into this brave new world: the potential *downside* of a too-great, or misconceived, emphasis on "Personalized Learning."

In reviewing the American "Silicon Valley" schools, in particular, there does not seem to be much direct attention paid to those overarching explanatory frameworks that might help locate an individual student's interests and aspirations within a larger human narrative. There is a whole lot of focus on the wants and needs of the individual learner, and not much on the legitimate aspirations of society as a whole.

TechCrunch writer Connie Loizos interviewed Paul France, a former Alt-School teacher, who has raised concerns about the brand of personalized learning that AltSchool and other newer schools are promoting.

"We live in this individualistic society that values personalized learning right now, almost to a fault. It's 'me, me, me.' But it's not a solution to any real problem in education."[19] France worries that "AltSchool and its ilk may be unwittingly hamstringing both students and teachers by both creating too much individualized content for students ('that's not how social systems or jobs work,' he notes) as well as unduly burdening teachers who are sometimes given unreal expectations to meet."[20]

"There's this assumption that every kid needs a different activity to meet their needs, and that by applying tech, one can simply send them individualized content through a video or activity card, but that's not necessarily true. It's not best for kids to learn only through a video or other content that's sent primarily for consumption. And tech that operates under this assumption really undermines educators and the value of good teaching."[21]

Educational critic Alfie Kohn has similar, and more specific, concerns:

"...much of what's marketed as 'personalized learning' amounts to little more than breaking knowledge and ideas down into 'itty-bitty parts,' then using extrinsic rewards to 'march kids through a series of decontextualized skills they had no meaningful role in choosing.'"[22]

In an *Education Week* article entitled, The Case(s) Against Personalized Learning, education commentator Benjamin Herold points to a different concern:

"...many critics worry that algorithms are increasingly being used to make key decisions shaping children's futures, without any real way for students or parents to understand how those choices are made, or challenge them for possible errors or biases."[23]

The caution for parents and educators alike, then, is to be on guard about a too narrow and too prescriptive version of personalized learning. If the vision is indeed to break down all knowledge and ideas into constituent parts to force feed students—admittedly, on a differential timing schedule—this could be soul-destroying. It is, once again, to narrow, fragment and trivialize the curriculum, albeit this time in digital form.

If, on the other hand, personalized learning is a mechanism that can better match instructional delivery with the differential learning styles and abilities of individual learners, and at the same time create opportunities for increased student agency over the grade school years, then it has something powerful to offer. The challenge in deploying personalized learning responsibly is to understand and use it as but one strategic technique embedded within a larger, more integrated, approach to education.

Possible Futures

Moving Forward

There is no reason, *in principle*, why public schools cannot be just as committed and innovative as the outlier schools in their pursuit of a remarkable education for kids. There is no reason, in principle, why the educational leaders, teachers and parents associated with public and conventional private schools cannot identify and embrace a powerful philosophy of what they are trying to accomplish in their schools and then use that philosophy to build the architecture to deliver on their goals. While skeptics might claim that there are many reasons, *in practice*, why this is impossible, the point of this book is to offer reasons why now might be precisely the time to actually change our practices.

I started my own independent school because I was *impatient* with what I took to be the lost potential of contemporary education. I know that there are plenty of parents, teachers, and educational leaders out there who are equally impatient. I think that now, more than ever, the time is right to open the lid on that big black box of education and see if we might re-examine and reconfigure what's inside.

That said, I am under no illusions about how difficult wholesale change might be. There are a number of challenges and tensions that will need to be worked through before any lasting transformation will see the light of day. What follows are some thoughts on just a few of these.

CLOSED OR OPEN?

There is, to begin with, a fundamental tension between a "top-down and closed" approach to educational system-making and one that is more "organic and open." In a top-down and closed approach, an external authority creates a prescribed curriculum and/or set of operations and then requires clients to adopt its prescriptions in total.

One example is when a Ministry of Education or State Department introduces and new program on high, without much previous consultation. Schools that expect their teachers to use proprietary software are another example of this. To some extent the International Baccalaureate Programme is likewise top-down and prescriptive, particularly the grade 11-12 Diploma Programme. An organic and open system, on the other hand, typically offers clients something more akin to a framework, and then invites them to fill in the spaces according to the unique needs and capacities of their local situation. Educational models that encourage schools and districts to use open source software are on the same wavelength.

I suspect that the "open framework" approach is likely the one to prevail, and likely the one with the most potential to create lasting educational improvements. In saying this, however, I am not calling for "a thousand points of light" where we invite would-be innovators to run off madly in all directions. I am saying instead that we need to begin with a framework that is steeped in clarity of purpose, so that the particular local strategies we select will all be aimed toward the same goal. "Steadfast in purpose, but agnostic in methodology" is likely the best way to proceed.

LEADERSHIP ON THE GROUND

Secondly, I suspect that we also need to find a way to move more educational responsibility and operational authority to the principals and education teams that actually run the schools.

Public school principals and the teachers they lead are often recipients of the next "best idea" from the Ministry of Education or the Superintendent's office, without having had much initial input into plans that are afoot. They typically have even less opportunity to determine how best to deploy these new ideas in the context of their particular community. This is a waste of talent because the public school principals I have met have more than enough intelligence, capacity, and desire to create remarkable educational experiences for students.

In the 1990s, there was a push in public education for what was called "site-based management." The basic idea, in theory, was "to transform schools into communities where the appropriate people participate constructively in major decisions that affect them".[1] The thought was to set up something like a site-based council that would have some combination of teachers, parents, community representatives, and the principal. The hope was that this arrangement would not only bring about improved "student achievement," but it would also create a strong sense of ownership and responsibility amongst the entire community associated with the school.

Some commentator reviews of site-based management at the time imply that, by and large, things did not go particularly well.[2] They cite the following reasons why many of these initiatives were unsuccessful:

- lack of clarity about which stakeholders (superintendent, principals, teachers, parents) should be responsible, and accountable, for which functions (budgeting, staff hiring and firing, curriculum, extra-curricular activities), which hampered a team's effectiveness
- lack of access to relevant information with which to make decisions
- lack of training, for principals, in "facilitative" leadership and, for all parties, in collaborative decision-making

- lack of long-term commitment from the central office to see these structural changes through

Detractors, including teacher unions[3], also identified their own causes for concern:

- that the site-based model, as adopted from the business world, is irrelevant in the context of public schools and, in any case, had been rejected by business
- that shifting accountability—particularly financial accountability—down" to schools relieves the central authorities of their responsibility to provide the public system with adequate funding
- that implementing a system of school-based budgeting, in particular, would threaten the principle of equity wherein each school gets what it needs to deliver quality education for all (e.g., a school with significant expenses supporting special needs students would be forced to cut other expenses elsewhere)
- that site-based management schemes which initially put a premium on decision-making by way of consultative teams of principals, teachers, and parents almost inevitably devolve into decision-making made primarily by the principal
- that the research is equivocal about the extent to which site-based management necessarily leads to gains in "student achievement"
- that site-based management diverts teachers and principals away from what matters most—their students and the quality of education at their schools—with principals spending their time ordering supplies rather than attending to their educational programs

Educational commentator Jane L. David observed in 1995 that:

> "Unfortunately, in practice, the potential of site-based management is rarely realized. It can even have deleterious effects, exhausting limited energy and goodwill in futile exercises."[4] Larry Kuehn, the then Director of Research and Technology of the British Columbia Teachers' Federation, likewise more directly proposed that "the reality does not match the rhetoric" when it comes to site-based management.[5]

To my way of thinking, the great thing about being able to examine an initiative like this in hindsight is to be able to use the mistakes of the past as a foundation to build a better model for the future. In her 1995 Educational Leadership article, Jane L. David already pointed the way to what needs to be in place for this kind of structural initiative to be successful:

- a well-thought-out committee structure (that is clear and sensible about which stakeholders would address what issues and whether their work yield formal approvals or informal advice)
- a substantive framework within which to make appropriate curricular choices
- strong principals (and sometimes teachers) who exercise leadership by being models of inquiry and reflection and who mobilize others to participate
- a concerted focus on the ultimate goal (i.e., by consciously connecting non-instructional decisions with conditions that maximize learning opportunities)
- a focus on research and evidence to determine what is, and what is not, working
- a principled commitment not to get caught up in details of management or curriculum or be waylaid by individual agendas
- access to relevant information for decision-making
- training and support in collaborative decision-making, facilitation, and mediation

A few additional observations of my own might be of use. The problem of ensuring proper funding equity had already been solved in the mid-1990s by Emery Dosdall, the superintendent of Edmonton Public Schools. His formula was to make per-student allocations on the basis of the number and categories of the students in schools.[6] The issue of principals getting diverted to administrative tasks like buying supplies can easily be solved by delegating those responsibilities to an office manager who works in concert with the central district.

Of perhaps more fundamental concern, however, is the nature of educational leadership—the leadership of the school principal, in particular—that is presupposed within most schemes of site-based management. The prevailing idea seems to be that school principals should exercise "facilitative" leadership, which seems to mean in part that they should help their team gain the necessary communication and decision-making skills to develop and implement a school-improvement plan. They should also disperse power responsibility.[7]

In trying to imagine how principals might actually be empowered to manage all of this in today's schools, it might be useful to take a page out the independent school's playbook. Most independent schools in Canada[8] are registered non-profit societies that are overseen by a Board of Governors that has only three main duties: to hire and fire the Head of School, to approve the school's budget, and to map out the long-term strategic future of the school. Board members usually consist of past and present parents, external community or professional members, and the Head of School. In this way, these boards—with two exceptions—are not dissimilar to the imagined site-based councils.

The first exception is that most Boards of Canadian independent schools do not typically have teachers as members. The second is that most Boards do not go anywhere near issues of curriculum. The reason for this is that they expect their Heads of School *themselves* to work effectively with teachers to develop and deliver the school's program. They expect their Heads of School, in other words, to be educational leaders.

One approach that I found helpful in allowing me to function as an educational leader in my own school was to make a clear distinction between the kind of conversation I was having with staff at each particular point in time. While the literature on site-based management seems to imagine a dichotomy where principals must be either "directive" or "facilitative," I think there is a valuable middle way.

I think there are, in fact, at least three kinds of conversation purposes that principals can have in speaking with staff: direction, consultation, and consensus. Directives can, and should, be used in those cases—like student safety—where the consequences and the justification are very straightforward. When we took our students on wilderness out-trips, there wasn't much debate about the protocols that needed to be in place.[9] In the early years of running the school, I spent quite a bit of time trying to achieve consensus among our staff about all sorts of things, including school culture and discipline. This would sometimes result in three hour after-school meetings that went around in circles and got nowhere.

Toward the latter half of my tenure, I switched over to the consultative approach. This enabled me to get genuine feedback from staff, but at the same time move things along in a timely fashion.

In a consultative approach, the principal makes clear to her staff that she is soliciting input on a particular *draft* proposal in much the same way that anyone might refer to a consultant to deepen and broaden their understanding of a particular issue. The key to a consultative relationship is that, at the end of the day, it is the "client"—in this case, the principal—who will make the final call on what exactly happens. The principal, however, is *genuinely* seeking the advice and perspective of the consultants—in this case, the teachers—because they have relevant expertise concerning at least some elements of the proposal. I have learned a few things in operating this way:

- It is usually better for the principal to bring a reasonably-developed draft plan to the table, rather than a poorly articulated and open-ended problem. I have found that staff usually appreciate something specific and concrete to respond to.

- This can't be a fake form of consultation wherein the principal has already made up their mind about an issue and simply makes a show of "asking for feedback" as an artificial exercise in building engagement. It needs to be a genuine consultation where a principal can, and should, amend elements of the plan based on relevant insights. (Where time permits, it is usually helpful to go a couple of rounds on a proposal.)

- It is helpful for the principal to be open and honest about some of the external structural challenges (e.g., funding, scheduling) that can work against, and sometimes defeat, a proposal.

In our school, I rarely engaged in directive conversations and almost never attempted consensus discussions.[10] Most of my interactions with staff concerning program and school culture were consultative. I found that our staff appreciated this way of operating for a number of reasons. Like most people, they do not want to spend their time in endless meetings that go nowhere. While they were committed to offering thoughtful input, they also liked the clarity and honesty of knowing who had the ultimate responsibility for making the final decision about the particular proposal under investigation.

In some staff rooms, there is much hand-wringing about "power" and who has what level of responsibility and accountability. I think that most teachers do not really want the "power" (and responsibility) to run an entire school. I think what they really want is to be listened to and have some opportunity to contribute to the improvement of what goes on in their school. They also want clarity about their own spheres of responsibility and accountability. For most teachers, the primary zone of responsibility in their minds is the learning and well-being of their own students.

Contrary, then, to principals having a merely "facilitative" role, I think they need to be seen as the educational leaders in their schools. That's what we pay them for. They need, to be sure, to be skilled at engaging teachers and parents (and students) in the important questions about how best to run their schools, but at the end of the day, it needs to be clearly understood that they are calling the shots.

RIGHT BALANCE

At Island Pacific School, we had a constant struggle trying to figure out how best to combine all the constituent elements of what we wanted to do with our students academically. On one hand, we wanted to make sure they had a firm grounding in the "basics" of any subject matter. We wanted them to learn their multiplication tables, to be able to read distance on a map, to know how to conduct and record a scientific experiment, and to be capable of writing grammatically correct sentences. We also wanted them to be able to demonstrate that they could use these basic operations in novel situations. (For example, use what you know about addition, division, and averages to figure out the average number of students in classes at the school.) But we wanted more: we wanted to find ways to have our kids truly internalize and appreciate what they learned by extending their explorations into areas of personal interest. We used individual and group projects as a mechanism to try and make this happen. And finally, above all of this, we also wanted our students to come away with a, perhaps nascent, understanding of how one particular investigation might fit within a larger intellectual exploration—or conversation, if you will.

We all knew of teachers who concentrate almost exclusively on "basic skills," leaving opportunities for creative exploration more or less in the margins. "Death by worksheet" is a common complaint in these sorts of classrooms. But there are also teachers who pride themselves on their project-based investigations of subject matter, who nonetheless offer learning experiences that can be wafer thin. There are lots of examples of students who enjoy making sugar cube pyramids or volcanoes but who have no idea what they are talking about. While most schools routinely attempt to have students apply what they know, we had less familiarity with other schools directly addressing the issue of big picture understanding.

Our challenge was to figure out how to understand and combine these constituent parts into a coherent whole. The goal was to do this in a way that would yield genuine understanding and engagement on the part of our students.

We eventually created an operational formula as follows:

CONTEXT + (BASELINE, APPLICATION, AND EXTENSION)

By "context" we meant an obligation on our part to continually find ways to locate our particular investigations within larger explanatory frameworks. In a wonderful book entitled *Small is Beautiful*, the political economist E.F. Schumacher wrote that:

> *"...we may be fortunate (if fortunate it is) and find a teacher who will 'clear our minds', clarify the ideas—the large and universal ideas already existent in our minds—and thus make the world intelligible for us."*[11]

It is this imperative to find ways to point students to those large and universal ideas that is crucial to having them understand their own learning in the context of broader human aspirations. If we do not consistently locate new ideas and operations within larger explanatory frameworks for students, we conceal from them those ongoing "great conversations" that thread through all the disparate people, events, inventions, works of art, and formulas that they may encounter. We fail, in other words, to connect the dots for our students. If, for example, in the context of a science class, students do not understand Isaac Newton's quote about "standing on the shoulders of giants," they do not really understand science. They may memorize (for a time) the elements of the periodic table or the parts of a cell, but they will never appreciate science as a particular way of seeing the world that depends on replicating results and building on the work of others.

Locating discrete subject matter within the context of a broader explanatory framework and broader human aspirations is but one necessary prerequisite to deep understanding and engagement. The other pieces—baseline, application, and extension—are equally important.

By "baseline," we meant those baseline literacy elements (knowledge and skills) that are the necessary operative parts at the core of any human undertaking. They include things like learning multiplication tables (math), understanding scale on a map (geography), practicing scales (music), cutting a straight line (carpentry), writing grammatically correct sentences (English), conjugating verbs (French), and identifying informal fallacies (practical reasoning). They also include a working understanding of the central concepts within different areas of investigation, for example mass, velocity (science); capital, income (economics); character, setting, plot, theme (literature); primary and secondary sources (history); and deductive, inductive arguments (practical reasoning). However identified and configured, these might be regarded as the "entrance level" requirements that need to be understood or otherwise mastered in order to participate within that particular domain.

The "application" phase of educative investigation is relatively straightforward: it is the place where one applies baseline knowledge and skills to some relevant investigation or activity. Upon learning, for example, that the area of a rectangle is determined by multiplying length times width, a simple application would be to then determine how much paint would be needed to cover a particular wall. So too with determining the distance between London and Paris; performing a musical piece; building a birdhouse; writing a position paper; speaking French; and constructing a defensible argument. The application phase simply puts to use the baseline literacy elements, but hopefully in a way that illustrates the utility, power, and beauty of the practice that is being investigated.

Notice that all of the "baseline" and most of the "application" elements are teacher-engineered, which means that the teachers have a clear idea of the elements they need their students to understand and a clear plan for introducing students to those elements (always encapsulated, it will be remembered, within the context of a larger explanatory framework). Notice as well that the expectation is that all students will achieve mastery at the baseline level, and that most students will demonstrate mastery or near-mastery when it comes to applications.

The "extension" phase of an investigation, however, is meant to be different on both counts. This is the place where the teacher needs to step back and offer a more or less open invitation to the student to use baseline and application learning to extend the investigation into an area of personal interest. While this typically might take the form of a project, it might also happen by way of a student deciding to challenge an external math competition. The ultimate extension at Island Pacific School was, of course, the Masterworks program. At the highest level, student agency is paramount, for in addition to allowing students to "play to their own strengths," these kinds of explorations encourage students to discover and develop their interests and abilities as an expression of their emerging self-determination.

The point of laying out the constituent elements of baseline, application and extension in this fashion is to begin to appreciate how these might be best combined. While some models of education over-emphasize baseline literacy by having students memorize facts devoid of context or application, others might run the risk of giving students all flash and no substance. The real challenge is to figure out the right balance of baseline, application, and extension so as to give students the kinds of explanatory frameworks that will serve as an invitation and a catalyst for their own exploration and expression of who they are.

THE RIGHT THING AT THE RIGHT TIME

The obvious complement to the principle of "Right Balance" is the principle that we need to do the "Right Thing at the Right Time." By this I mean that we need to have a coherent picture in our minds about the contribution that each level of schooling—elementary, middle, high school—could and should make to a student's overall education. I think there are important distinctions to be made here, for example, about the relative balances of baseline, application, and extension in each of these levels. I also think that if we can become clearer and more intentional about these sorts of things, we will be more effective at each level, and each level will build upon and reinforce the others.

In trying to make sense of this, it is perhaps useful to imagine a rough and ready matrix to distinguish the different priorities and purposes of each level. Elementary school, for example, lays a strong foundation for students, middle school can be a time of guided exploration, while the high school years provide an opportunity to attempt an initial consolidation for students as follows:

- Elementary (Foundation)
- Middle School (Guided Exploration)
- High School (Consolidation)

Before commenting on the K-12 levels proper, it is important to recognize and appreciate the absolutely crucial work of early childhood educators—those pre-school and special service providers who serve families with children from ages 0-5. Working together with parents, they help nurture the monumental social and developmental growth that is happening over these early years. Their work provides the preconditions for everything that follows.

In proposing that the elementary school years (age 6-10) provide a "foundation" for students in the context of grade school, I mean partially that these are the years in which students must acquire the kind of knowledge, skills, and dispositions that will give them the capacity for further learning. These include reading, writing, and the ability to perform basic mathematical calculations, but they also include initial exposure to myriad explanatory lenses—the socio-political constructs of space (geography) and time (history), for example—upon which subsequent understanding can build.

Using the language of liberal education, I would once again describe some of what students need to learn here as *emancipatory competencies*—the skills and dispositions that will eventually enable them to be free in the sense of having the ability to create a worthwhile life narrative for themselves.

The elementary school years are also the years where students first encounter and negotiate sustained social interactions outside the family. One of the key roles of the elementary school educator is to set the norms of what will count as acceptable and unacceptable behaviour, at least within the context of a classroom. This is a very tricky business because the teacher has to create, communicate, and enforce some very basic norms having to do with safety and fundamental respect, all the while being careful not to offend individual parents' sensibilities about these sorts of things. Tricky or not, this socialization component is central to what both early educators and elementary school teachers routinely do.

As discussed earlier, we created Island Pacific School because we knew that the greatest challenge in *the middle years* (ages 11-14) is to sustain and enhance intellectual curiosity in young people. In elementary school, most students have a kind of innocent and natural curiosity and are therefore willing and receptive (for the most part) to engage in new learning. When students hit the middle years, however, they can "flatline" in terms of their intellectual curiosity and engagement. One of the biggest reasons for this is that they shift their focus of interest and attention from ideas and discoveries to social interactions with their peers.

The challenge in the middle years, therefore, is to create the kind of guided explorations they need to eventually find their own voice. We created a very intentional middle school educational community at IPS because we knew we needed to get this right. We also knew that if we failed to pay attention to the middle years, we could lose the opportunity for learning, engagement, and growth crucial to further development. This is the central test of middle school, the challenge that needs to be overcome in any transformation of the system as a whole.

The "consolidation" function that I imagine for high school gets realized on two different fronts. On one level, students should eventually come to get an initial glimpse of the underlying patterns and interconnections within human inquiry—as Schumacher hopes, to make the world intelligible by clarifying those "large and universal ideas already existent in our minds." On a second level, however, there should come about some initial consolidation, some personal clarity, about who one is as an individual—what they are interested in, what they are passionate about, and what they stand for. The problem, of course, with implying that each educational stage should be dedicated to a single imperative (Foundation, Guided Exploration, and Consolidation) is that all stages truly need to have some constant combination of all three. While the emphasis in the elementary years might be on "Foundations," opportunities for exploration and consolidation should be welcomed and exploited when they occur.

That said, there is something intuitively obvious about the idea that students should have a strong foundation so that their subsequent explorations can be fruitful, so that eventually they have the capacity to attempt certain kinds of consolidations, and indeed the capacity to discover their own strengths and passions.

With regard to the question of right balance of, for example, baseline, application, and extension, it follows that the relative proportions of these three content elements should change over the different levels of schooling. A rough approximation might look like this:

ELEMENTARY (Foundation)

Baseline	Application	Extension

MIDDLE YEARS (Guided Exploration)

Baseline	Application	Extension

HIGH SCHOOL (Consolidation)

Baseline	Application	Extension

One key idea here is, again, the importance of being intentional about increasing *student agency* as learners progress through the different levels. If the goal is to set students up to cultivate their humanity, and one component of that involves enabling them to pursue the question "What are my interests, abilities, and passions?" we need to systematically build in more opportunities for serious personal inquiry.

The other implication is that if we become clearer about the different proportions that might be appropriate for the different levels, we can become more focused and effective at each of our respective levels. If I know that elementary school teachers are doing a rock-solid job of foundations (both personal and academic), I will have the capacity to pursue some of those all-important guided explorations in the middle years. Similarly, if high school instructors and counsellors know that the middle years students have been given a strong foundation that includes the capacity to ask intelligent questions, they know they will have the license to push students to define for themselves the kinds of pursuits they need to investigate.

At IPS, we learned that to do the "right thing at the right time" in the context of the overarching goal to equip and inspire students to cultivate their humanity required that we simultaneously look at the forest *and* the trees. We needed to pay attention to the social and developmental needs of the middle school students in our care, but we also needed to understand their potential as contributing adults to the world at large. This is just one of the many things that parents and educators need to keep in mind when contemplating a new education system for the next generation.

Possible Futures

High School Reimagined: Program Elements

It seems to me that the best way to reconstruct grade school education in total is to start at the end, with high school. If we can create a picture in our mind of where we want our senior students to be in terms of their understanding, abilities, and intellectual and social maturity, we will be in a better position to more appropriately engineer both the elementary and middle school experiences for students.

In the next two chapters, I will sketch out a rough example of what one high school environment might look like. This chapter will describe the core elements of the model, while the chapter following will offer a "Day in the Life" narrative of what this might look like from a student's point of view.

THE BASIC IDEA: INTEGRATING ELEMENTS

We need to stop seeing schooling—and high school in particular—as a set of discrete courses that need to be completed within a particular timetable. Instead, it should be seen as an interlocking series of educational elements specifically designed to directly address fundamental purposes.

Some of these elements will target baseline understanding of specific knowledge domains, while others will enable students to eventually "connect the dots" to appreciate subjects as great conversations. Some will invite students to pursue individual passions, while others will compel them to investigate unexplored terrain. Some will confront students with personal challenges, while others will allow them to play to their strengths.

For some of these elements it will make sense to participate in more or less the same age groupings; for others, it will not. Some will be undertaken individually; others will be conducted in partnerships or teams.

It will be the careful integration of these elements, however, that will matter most. For a genuine education to emerge, the program must be designed so that the whole becomes greater than the sum of its parts.

What follows is a sample list of core elements that could go into the mix.

START-UP WORKSHOPS

We waste a lot of time in schools. We sometimes drag things along endlessly over an entire term of classes. Or worse, we sometimes intend to address something throughout the year but end up losing the thread in the turmoil of competing demands.

Take, for example, English grammar. Most English teachers feel they have some obligation to teach English grammar in some form over the course of an instructional year, but for many it is not their favourite thing to do. They would prefer to arrange book circles for students or have them write interesting stories. The bare rudiments of sentence structure, however, are not that difficult to teach. This is the kind of thing that can be introduced in two to three start-up workshops at the beginning of the year and then be consistently followed up in all written presentations by the entire staff.

Introductory workshops at the beginning of the year can serve a broader purpose: they can lay the groundwork for the investigative and exploratory challenges that will form the bulk of a student's program throughout the year. They are an excellent place to introduce some of those "21st century learning skills" as one component of a student's total education. Imagine starting the year with a short series of workshops on the following themes:

Executive functioning strategies. This would cover time management, advance planning, and strategies to avoid becoming distracted. In any school, students get distracted all the time. In a more open-scheduled learning environment, such as the one that I propose, students will have even more opportunities to be distracted and not make the best use of their time. However, if we equip them up front with strategies to keep themselves on track, they will get a lot more out of their year.

Working effectively in groups. One of the worst experiences a student can have is to participate in a so-called "group project" where one student does the bulk of the heavy lifting, while the others assemble simple graphics or do nothing at all. Working well as a team is actually a sophisticated undertaking. The workshops would teach students about defining clear roles and responsibilities at the outset and identifying accountability benchmarks as the project progresses. Students could also be introduced to the concept of design thinking in those cases where the exploration calls for a new solution to a problem.

Effective internet searches. Most students are not particularly sophisticated in the way they search the internet and are unaware of some of the more powerful search engines available. Hardly any know how to employ filters effectively and can waste hours going down irrelevant rabbit holes. Understanding how to conduct searches right from the get-go will prove invaluable.

Building an "internet toolkit." This would explain how to assemble a set of useful online resources that students can, and should, turn to as they make their way through the rest of the program. I have found that middle school students, at least, are remarkably unaware of basic resources like dictionary sites, historical timelines and digital atlases.

When the intent is to set students up at the beginning of the year for the challenges and opportunities that will follow, any number of preparatory workshops will be useful for different levels of students at different times. (This is likely a good place, for example, for the obligatory session on proper citation of references.) The point is to introduce students to essential tools and pre-requisite soft skills early, so they are well-equipped to get the most out of their program over the remainder of the year.

ONLINE PROGRAMS FOR BASELINE LITERACY

The beginning of the year is also the time to introduce students to a set of serviceable online learning platforms that will help them acquire, over the course of the year, a *baseline literacy* understanding of key areas of inquiry, including math, science, and history. In math, for example, they might move back and forth between the Khan Academy and Math IXL as suits their ability. In science, there are endless possibilities, including everything from basic programs like those created by Time 4 Learning[1] to more sophisticated programs created by textbook companies like Pearson[2]. For history, students could be introduced to several timeline platforms[3] and video playlists[4] as baseline resources to gain a better understanding of the human story. This would also be a good time to introduce students to a second language platform that will form one part of their second language acquisition progression.[5]

One of the advantages of having students use these kinds of programs is that they can do so at their own pace, regardless of their age. Some are also designed with feedback algorithms calibrated to provide just the right follow-up challenges to ensure maximum learning. With a multitude of programs out there and more being developed all the time, there are good opportunities to find the right fit for each student.

These programs should be understood as being, at best, a single thread in a multi-weave tapestry. Their purpose and scope is simply to provide a vehicle through which students can gain access to a baseline literacy understanding of a form of knowledge. While they will augment a student's total education, they certainly do not define it. Our experience at IPS and emerging research suggests that students should spend no more than 10-25% of their time using these kinds of programs.

These introductory workshops and online learning platforms are simply the preliminary structural pieces that set students up for the heart of their educational experience: "Investigations," "Explorations," and "Practices."

INVESTIGATIONS COURSES

We have all had them. Those teachers who somehow manage to suck us into a subject area, pursuit, or way of thinking that we simply would not have encountered on our own. They usually do it by way of a deft combination of raw competence, passion, and storytelling. In the first instance, these are the teachers who know their stuff; they are not faking it. Their competence, however, is simply an expression of their passion; they know their terrain because they love it. They are usually a little crazy in their excitement about what they know, and that enthusiasm rubs off on their students. And they typically like to tell stories, sometimes about themselves, but more often about the new universe into which they have invited you. The effect on you as a student is profound. You dive deep into the material because you have an undefined sense there are important reasons for doing so. In some inchoate way this pursuit links you as an individual to something larger than yourself.

The teacher I most remember was Ken Coates, a Canadian history professor teaching a second-year undergraduate university course. The subject matter was dense to say the least, for he gave us layer upon layer of fact, context, situation, influence, and story. The net effect on me, however, was a much deeper appreciation not only for the Canadian story but also for the complexity of any history.

A key challenge in reconfiguring education lies in encouraging teachers to do a very particular job with students: investigate science, mathematics, technology, philosophy, religion, the arts, and the humanities in a way that enables students—all students—to connect the dots between isolated facts and the deeper conversations in which they are embedded. The task, in fact, is to have students discover the lineage and explanatory power of some of the greatest intellectual and creative achievements of humanity in a way that will eventually serve as an inspiration and conceptual foundation for their own explorations. These investigations furnish both the context and the rationale for the baseline literacy competencies first encountered in the online programs.

What we are after, therefore, is a 21st century version of a survey course that has the capacity to engage, at different levels and in different ways, both middle and high school students. We want the kind of courses that explore discoveries, works of art, and ideas as exemplars of human ingenuity and creativity, and at the same time elements of an ongoing and sometimes contradictory "great conversation" of human inquiry. Think of the content within those remarkable BBC documentaries like Kenneth Clark's *Civilization*, Jacob Bronowski's *Ascent of Man,* and James Burke's *Connections*. Now imagine that we can transform and make accessible that content to adolescent minds. This is a tall order to be sure, but not impossible.

Take, for example, the online *Crash Course History*[6] series hosted by John Green and available on YouTube and through the Khan Academy. This is a funny, irreverent, and content rich exploration of world history that would likely appeal to a young audience. (The excerpt at the beginning of this book that confronts the question, "Will this be on the test?" is from the beginning of the first episode of that series.) There is no reason why gifted teachers can't use these kinds of resources to offer students an accessible gateway to create a rich understanding of the world.

EXPLORATIONS

Explorations is the name given to a designated "playlist" of exploratory pro-jects that students would complete, sometimes in concert with their Investi-gations courses, as part of their overall educational plan. They would come in two forms: Challenges or Discoveries.

Challenges are tightly-designed learning tasks that require students to solve a closely-defined problem. Although some of these might be fairly short and confined explorations, others will be more expansive. Some Challenges will be subject specific, but most will be interdisciplinary in nature. One chal-lenge, for example, might be "The Secrets of the Great Pyramid," wherein students need to figure out the contents (and value) of potential treasure located in the pyramid and then draw up a plan for its retrieval. This will require a combination of historical research, mathematical calculation, phys-ics (to determine how to move massive blocks), planning, and presentation (i.e., a written report). In most cases, the Challenges would require applica-tion of skills or concepts already learned, but in some cases, they might re-quire new learning. The objective in all cases is to solve a predefined problem.

Discoveries, on the other hand, would be more open-ended. They might include an invitation to "research and report" on selected topics, or to "cre-ate and present" using selected media. They are more like the kinds of things that the students at High Tech High pursue. A good example of a Dis-covery undertaking would also be the individual Masterworks projects that are currently completed at Island Pacific School.

Students would be expected to complete a progression and set number of Challenges and Discoveries according to their ever-evolving educational plan. Note that while many of these projects would be done individually, some would need to be completed in pairs or teams, a few of which would include cross-age groupings.

The whole point of Explorations—whether Challenges or Discoveries—is to create a built-in opportunity for students to apply and extend what they are learning by way of the other elements. This is the place for full hands-on engagement, where students confront challenges and make discoveries in a progression that is fine-tuned to both their needs and interests.

PRACTICES

Practices are those things that a balanced, creative, compassionate, and intellectually curious human being cultivates on a regular basis. These are things like reading for pleasure, being physically active, paying attention to what is happening in the world, finding contemplative space, helping others, making something, and expanding one's base of knowledge and ability.

The challenge within the context of grade-school education is how to encourage these attributes in a way that is meaningful for students and that might lead them to incorporate them into their everyday lives. The solution is to build these elements into the very fabric of the place so that reading, physical activity, creativity, service, and thoughtful reflection are both habitual and commonplace. The way to do that is to be intentional about creating the structures that encourage and express these attributes.

These could include the following:

Book Groups

It is a challenge, sometimes, to get students to read, particularly in this age of instantaneous media. In the absence of direct brain infusions, however, reading is still the gateway to an infinite world of learning and experience. This is as much the case for expository works (that might explain how an airplane flies) as it is for literature. The difficulty, though, is to cultivate a genuine love of reading across a broad swath of learners, all with varying abilities and interests. One solution is to borrow from the adult concept of book clubs by creating a network of "Book Groups" to which students would sign up as members, based on their interests and reading level. Although they would be led by a facilitator, the real object would be to orchestrate a focused discussion amongst all participants in the group.

The proposition here is that if student readers have the opportunity to talk together about the books they read in a non-threatening and supportive environment, they might gradually broaden the range of their interests and their capacity and pleasure in reading. From a program point of view, there could be a list of required core readings to be encountered at some point over the middle and high school programs. Each student's progress could be tracked with a view to steadily enhance their reading ability and interest and at the same time expose them to seminal works. The goal would be to make sure that each student regards him or herself as a reader by the time they leave the program.[7]

Physical Activity Requirement

If the object of our efforts truly is to equip and inspire students to cultivate their humanity, we need to pay attention to the physical activity of our students. A healthy body helps sustain a healthy mind. To work through introductory workshops, be attentive and engaged during Book Group meetings, get the most out of the Investigations courses, and invest oneself fully in the Exploration projects requires an acuity of mind that cannot help but be enhanced by the right balance of physical activity.

The challenge is that physically active people already know this, while people who are not physically active still need to learn it. What our full cohort of learners needs is a physical activity requirement that celebrates the active students and inspires the couch potatoes.

It needs to start with a rationale. I am often surprised by how little respect we show our students by failing to give them any reasons or justifications for the things we think they should do. We seem to think that by simply announcing something as a "requirement" is justification enough that it ought to be done. Worse still, we have whole generations of students who have been so habituated to not receiving justifications for things that they have come not to expect these. And while this may be efficient in the sense that most of them, by and large, do what they are told, the fatal downside here is that when something is an external requirement, it can (and does) get jettisoned at the first opportunity for free and individual choice. What we want to celebrate or, if necessary, *cultivate* over these pre-adult years, however, is a sustained commitment to physical activity over the course of an entire life. It is for this reason that a compelling rationale for sustained physical activity—in terms that they can understand—needs to come first.

The mechanics of setting up a flexible, yet substantive, physical activity "program" for a broad range of participation types would be reasonably straightforward. In conjunction with a suitable advisor, each student would be expected to create something like a Personal Activity Plan for the term or the year. For students who are already heavily involved in sports or special-ized training, this would mostly be a matter of identifying (and acknowledg-ing) what they are already doing. For those who participate in little to no physical activity, however, the job of the Advisor would be to co-create a manageable plan with the student. This might involve individual pursuits (such as swimming or going to the gym) or group activities such as recrea-tional sports team or dance classes. There would also be an accountability mechanism whereby the student (and advisor) would track the student's completion of the various activities and their growth throughout the plan.

The responsibility of the school or collegiate would be to ensure that there are enough activities available for the full range of their students' interests. It is likely that the school or collegiate would offer recreational sports teams, running clubs, and other opportunities. At the same time, some physical activity should occur outside the school—at community recreation centres, dance studios, sports leagues, swimming pools, or martial arts classes, for example, to reinforce the idea of lifelong participation in a healthy lifestyle.

The school would also augment the student's individualized programs by sponsoring single-issue seminars on physical health and fitness-related topics, which could include drug and alcohol education and the prevention of sexually transmitted diseases. Some of these would be mandatory. The overall goal is to give students an "Owner's Manual" orientation to the human body that will set them up for the rest of their lives.

World Watch Discussion Groups

We once had a humanities teacher at Island Pacific School who conducted "World Watch" discussions with students. Essentially, all she did was draw the students' attention to what was going on in the world and then ask them what they thought. She did this in such a passionate and informed way, however, that for many students, this was their first introduction to the world beyond their own noses.

I think that, under the right initial tutelage, something like the same investigative passion could be cultivated amongst our 15- to 17-year-old emerging adults. The challenge is to do this in a way where the students themselves eventually become the natural drivers of the inquiry. The key is to create a relatively informal structure wherein a skilled facilitator offers content, support, and guidance only as necessary, calibrated according to the maturity of the group.

I imagine, in other words, a group of 8-12 students meeting in person once a week for 30-45 minutes to discuss world affairs. The job of the facilitators would be to set an initial structure and co-create with the students a mechanism for ensuring everyone gets to contribute. While he or she might initially bring content to the table as a catalyst to get the group started, the goal would be to transfer the discussion to the students themselves. Along the way, the facilitator might model a certain style of inquiry (e.g., questions supported by substantive content within the stories, observations linked to related issues, or references to historical or literary parallels) as an implicit invitation to deepen and enrich the tenor of the conversation. The facilitator would also help the group through whatever obstacles they may encounter, be these interpersonal challenges or existential roadblocks (for example,

"With so many "bad" things happening in the world, what can we possibly do?").

Think of this as a mini "salon." Students might bring different items to the table based on their particular interests: business, science, art, politics, sports, etc. Or, the groups are perhaps reconfigured every few months to bring fresh perspectives into the conversations. Whatever the format, the point is to create a natural environment for students to investigate the world around them as part of the larger project of eventually figuring out where they might fit in.

Lend a Hand; Make a Difference

One of the additional elements most educators want to include in a menu of "good things" that we ought to do with students is provide some provision or mechanism that encourages them to make a positive contribution to their community or the world as a whole. The challenge is to find an authentic way to do this that goes beyond invoking mandatory "community service hours" and involves more than padding a resume for university admissions or future employment.

This goes back, once again, to establishing an authentic culture within a learning community. It is done by introducing or reconfirming the value and importance of a "lend a hand/make a difference" ethic, providing opportunities and encouragement for people to follow-through on that ethic, and then publicly supporting and acknowledging when people do so.

Here is a model for what that might look like:

- First, at the student orientation sessions at the beginning of the year, this ethic would be introduced as something worthwhile that everyone ought to pursue. It would be made clear that this is not something is done "for marks" or for credits but instead as an indication of one's maturity as a person. There would be an invitation, in other words, for the students to express the very best of who they are.

- Second, each student's assigned advisor (see below) would be the "on the ground" conduit for the encouragement of this ethic. During their regular check-in sessions, he or she would make a point of asking how their charges are "lending a hand or making a difference" in their lives.
- Third, the advisor would acknowledge and record each student's contributions.
- Finally, the schools would make a point of profiling other remarkable people outside the school who contribute to their local or global community in a positive way. These individuals might be part of a speaker series that provides at least some of the inspiration within the "equip and inspire" mandate of a quality education.

The point is that the cultivation of this ethic is so important that it cannot be left to artificial devices. It is an ethic that needs to permeate the entire ethos of the place, and it is something that is likely "caught" rather than "taught."

The Arts

Are the arts central to our humanity; do they partially define what it is to be a human being? Yes, of course. Is engagement in the arts worthwhile? Are there lessons in the arts—about persistence, humility, and the fruits of labour—that can be carried over to other aspects of a person's life? Is there an intrinsic good there? Yes again, on all counts.

Is engagement in the arts therefore something that needs to be included in one's formal education? Almost certainly, but once again the challenge is to arrange this in a way that allows for or actually cultivates an authentic embrace of an artistic sensibility within a broad range of students, many—or most—of whom would likely not describe themselves as "artistic."

Perhaps we need to start by redefining what could be meant by "the arts." Traditionally, we think of this category as encompassing the visual arts, music, literature, drama, film, and dance. In an educative context, however, it is useful to extend this definition to embrace any kind of *disciplined passion* that requires technique and rigor and evokes a certain amount of creativity. These "disciplined passions" might therefore include things like computer programming, boat building, interior design, fashion design, or landscaping. The idea here is to have the students find something that they can call their own, something that goes beyond describing what they do and instead defines who they are. Ideally, this pursuit should be something that requires persistence, skill, technique, and rigor that nonetheless allows for, and in fact requires, individual creativity.

The role of the school or collegiate would be similar to its role in encouraging the "lend a hand/make a difference" ethic: to set the norm that one should cultivate a passion or interest, to build in a mechanism to express that passion, and to create opportunities to showcase and celebrate student work. While the most obvious vehicle through which to do that would be by way of the individual explorations, other venues should be created as well.

This is why the school or collegiate should have an art gallery or presentation space to feature student work. This is also why, ideally, there should be an art and design workshop, a theatre space, a film studio, and a recording suite to provide the infrastructure for good things to happen. Our schools and collegiates should be constantly abuzz with expositions, concerts, film screenings, dance, and performances. The High Tech High "exhibitions" provides a good example of what this could look like.[8]

The point of creating a learning environment that includes things like book clubs, physical activity opportunities, world-watch discussion groups, design studios, and service experiences is to deepen and enrich the total educational experience. Without a consistent effort on our part to encourage the practices that emerge within these spaces and activities, we sell our students short; we fail to create the conditions to enable them to cultivate their humanity. With the active pursuit of these practices in place, we open doors to much broader landscapes.

TWO MORE PIECES

Two more components are needed to leverage and integrate this model of high school education most effectively.

The first of these is a customizable digital repository of every educative interaction, artifact, or achievement experienced or produced by a student. There are already many partial approximations of these kinds of repositories. AltSchool and Summit Schools have created their own in-house platforms, while the traditional textbook companies are also expanding in this direction.[9] What I imagine is something much larger: a giant personal learning map or matrix that captures and records inputs from the entire spectrum of the program, including progress and achievement in introductory workshops, online learning platforms, Investigations courses, and exploratory projects as well as evidence of books read, sculptures created, physical activity pursued, world watch commentary contributed, and community service rendered. This, in effect, becomes an ever-evolving learning and engagement profile that can be used to identify individual strengths and challenges, and thereby point the way for future planning. As mentioned in the section on student assessment, it also provides the foundation to create a deeper, richer, and more nuanced description of a student's interest and abilities.

The second and most important element that needs to be in place would be the inclusion of something like a personal tutor or program advisor as the centerpiece of the entire structure. Meeting with the student on a weekly or bi-weekly basis, this person would ideally become a kind of mentor with a responsibility to simultaneously pay attention to two different mandates. On one hand, she would serve as a program leader to guide the student through a set of rich educational experiences designed to expose students to the responsibilities and capacities of what it is to be a human being. On the other hand, he must act as a protective custodian perfectly attuned to the particular passions and potential of his individual charge. While this tutor, or mentor, or program advisor—call it what you will—would make frequent and intelligent use of the student's personal learning map to chart the next course, he or she would also (more importantly) take special care to know the student as a complete person.

THE SECRET SAUCE

Finally, every school needs its own "secret sauce"—those unique practices or program elements that embody the values it sets out to inculcate. One of the most straightforward ways to develop this sauce is to leverage the opportunities and experience of the community in which the school resides. The educative potential of a First Nations community, for example, is just as powerful as the untapped resources that might be harnessed in an inner-city school or a suburban community. The trick is to discover the resources that are available and then find a way to build the lessons they yield into the very fabric of the school.

At Island Pacific School, our secret sauce was more like a bouillabaisse—a combination of many bits and pieces. Certainly, we leveraged the opportunities and experience of our community. We took our kids on kayaking and hiking trips because the wilderness was more or less out our back door, and we drew on the passion and expertise of volunteer adults to serve on our Masterworks Committees. But it was also a combination of many little things: the way that the students stood up at the beginning of each class and took turns cleaning the school, and the way that parents would roll up their sleeves and take on countless volunteer jobs to make things run smoothly. Most important was the way that teachers would take extra time to check in on the kids to make sure they were okay.

The point is that—in addition to all the other elements outlined above—each school also needs to figure out for itself what distinctive programs or practices it is going to adopt to signal its key priorities.

HIGH SCHOOL REIMAGINED

The proposition being offered here is that if we reimagine the equivalent of high school education in this way, we will create an environment that demands more rigor and engagement of students but at the same time offers more authenticity, agency, and even joy. In graphic form, the various components must be represented as follows:

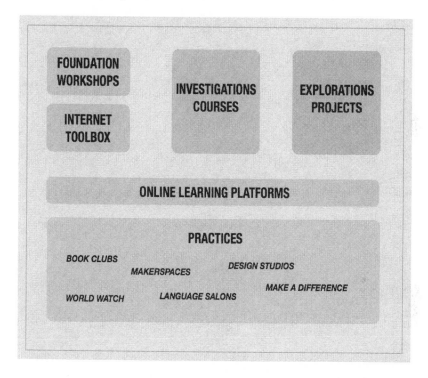

Clearly there are a lot of moving parts here, not all of which could likely be implemented within existing schools. Teachers and educational leaders will need to determine for themselves which elements might work within their own situation. The point for the time being, however, is to start becoming very intentional about how all the constituent parts are meant to contribute to a total educational experience that is worthy of our students' capacity and aspirations.

In the chapter that follows, I will offer a fictional "Day in the Life" overview of what this might look like from a student's point of view.

Possible Futures

High School Reimagined: A Day in the Life

IMAGINE THIS...

On Thursday, October 15th, 16-year-old Jennifer Wilson rises from bed, brushes her teeth, grabs a quick breakfast, and heads out the door for school. First stop is a local coffee shop where she meets with her World Watch group to catch up on unfolding events around the world. This cluster of eight students has been meeting for over a year now and have developed their own way—sometimes humorous, sometimes fiercely argumenta-tive—of investigating world events. The tutor who once led the discussion now interjects only occasionally to provide background information or fill in gaps. The group meets once a week, usually at a coffee shop, and usually first thing in the morning. Jennifer makes sure that she checks in to at least two news feeds before these sessions so that she is not out of the loop.

Thirty-five minutes later, Jennifer heads to her workspace at Urban Pacific Collegiate, located about 30 minutes by bus (and 20 minutes by bicycle) from her home. Irreverently referred to as "The Box," the Collegiate is a converted warehouse with two auditoriums, numerous large and small meeting rooms, an open-air learning commons and art gallery, a fitness room, an art & de-sign studio, a cafeteria, and workspaces for 350 students. Each workspace is a cubicle measuring about two meters by two meters with an adjustable desk, a chair or stool, a locker, a large bulletin board, and a power source. Students decorate and/or accessorize their spaces as they see fit.

Because she has completed all her "Core Skills Development" refresher workshops over the first five weeks of the year, Jennifer is eager to shift attention to the other elements of her program. The Core Skills workshops are universally known as "boot camp" courses because students have to master them in order to proceed. Like most of her colleagues, Jennifer grudgingly regards them as a necessary evil. They cover things like basic mathematics, grammar and sentence structure, expository writing, the fundamentals of rhetoric, reading for comprehension, and an introduction to reasoning. Jennifer found her entry year the hardest. She could not write a grammatically correct sentence to save her life, never mind a coherent blog or essay. But with many revisions and a lot of concentrated help, she eventually got the hang of it. She now finds the refresher courses much easier and—if she is honest with herself—even satisfying.

This morning, she wants to continue working on one of her "Investigations" courses. These are the teacher-led courses that survey the central discoveries, ideas, and events of science, history, philosophy, religion, art, literature, music, and technology in order to help Jennifer see connections within the "great conversations" of human inquiry. Although she has the option of taking these courses in a "full support," "variable support," or "independent" format, for this one she has chosen to be completely independent.

She spends the next hour and a half working through the taped presentations, watching the videos, reading the text, flipping through the photo galleries, completing the activities, and then taking the baseline comprehension quizzes to track her progress. She will also complete a group project related to the course. She will take three of these courses every year, some in a study group with full support, others with drop-in help, and others completely on her own. Although she knows that she needs to meet a set number of requirements to earn her formal "standing granted" for this course, she likes the flexibility of being able to do it on her own time in her own way.

With an hour to go before lunch, Jennifer decides to hit the gym. At the beginning of the year, her Physical Activity Coordinator had laid out a number of options as to how she could meet or exceed the minimum requirement of three hours a week of physical activity. Like a lot of students, Jennifer already had her own sports and training schedule, so this was not a difficult target for her to hit. For the moment, Jennifer's plan is to spend two hours a week working out in the gym and another hour a week playing badminton on Thursday evenings.

After her workout, Jennifer meets her friends for lunch in a nearby park. They are a multi-aged group of kids who are drawn together mostly by their love of film. They could spend hours debating which director is the best for dramas or which actor nailed a particular role. Jennifer is keen to hear what the group thinks of her ideas for a film she is working on because she is meeting with her Masterworks advisors on this topic right after lunch.

Within the collegiate program architecture, each student is expected to complete a series of "Exploration" projects every year. These might be teacher-directed assignments linked to courses and/or identified fields of study ("Challenges"), or student-designed pursuits completed individually or in small groups ("Discoveries"). The most extensive "Discoveries" are the Masterworks projects. In these, the students select a topic of personal interest and then work with an advisory committee to research, develop, and ultimately present their work to a public audience. The year-one Masterworks projects are fairly basic, with plenty of guidance and support from the Collegiate tutors. The year-two projects are more ambitious, and make some use of external advisors, while the year-three presentations are often outstanding.

At 1:00, Jennifer meets with her Masterworks Advisory Committee in a small meeting room that she has booked. She has three people on her committee: Alison McPherson, her chair who is a tutor at the Collegiate; Peter Kayle, a local documentary film director; and Philip Tsai, another documentary film director. Alison and Peter are there in person, while Philip joins the group via a video-conferencing platform. Jennifer wants to put together a short, 8-minute documentary on the plight of people living on the streets in the roughest part of town. She wants to pitch some ideas to her committee and get some advice about how best to proceed. They spend about an hour giving her some direction and a list of things she needs to have done by their next meeting in three weeks' time. Armed with new ideas, Jennifer goes back to her workspace and spends the next hour and a half working on a draft storyboard. She also fires off a few texts to her friends to see if she can line them up for filming. She has to hustle, though, to make it to a meeting with her "PA" (program advisor) at 3:30.

These PA meetings happen twice a month, or more frequently if needed, and are designed to make sure that students are on track and getting the support they need to complete their programs. Jennifer's PA is Geoff Maunder. Jennifer sometimes finds him a bit brusque, but he is always thorough. Geoff has a complete overview of Jennifer's progress to date in all elements of the program. He also has a weekly and monthly timetable that they have both worked out in previous meetings.

Geoff begins by congratulating Jennifer on doing so well in her Core Skills workshops. He notes that her enhanced writing ability is starting to show up in her project submissions. Geoff then asks whether Jennifer's decision to complete her Investigations course independently is actually working. He notes that Jennifer is not as far along as she should be and suggests that she switch to variable support for that course. Jennifer says she would rather try to stick it out as an independent student for the next month and decide at that point if she should change. Geoff grumbles a bit and makes a note to check in with Jennifer again on this in a week.

Geoff notes that Jennifer has been an avid participant in the World Watch meetings. He also says that Jennifer has done a good job of keeping up with her Physical Activity plan. He asks Jennifer what she has arranged for next term and recommends that she go and see the Physical Activity Coordinator to explore different possibilities, perhaps a team sport.

Geoff then asks Jennifer if she is keeping up with her "Book Group" reading. Jennifer is currently working her way through a required reading of Jane Austen's Pride and Prejudice and is due to meet with her book group tomorrow. She confesses that she will have to read 40 pages tonight to be ready for her session the next day.

Geoff moves on to ask Jennifer how she plans to arrange her "culture shock exploration" this year. In this new program introduced only at this school, students are expected to put themselves in a position in which they see the world from a perspective different from their own. Some students are investigating different religious beliefs, some spend time volunteering in soup kitchens, and some see what it is like going without sight or hearing for a couple of days. Last year, Jennifer spent a week living by day in the roughest part of her own city. (The journal that resulted gave her the idea for her Masterworks documentary.) This year, she would very much like to travel abroad, but realizes she does not yet have the funds to make that happen. Geoff recommends a few foundations to which she can apply for financial aid and also lets her know that a part-time position has come up in the cafeteria.

Geoff continues by asking Jennifer what she wants to do for her "Lend a Hand; Make A Difference" contribution this year. Jennifer reminds him that she is volunteering from 9:00-10:00am on Tuesday mornings at a daycare for hearing-impaired children, and Geoff adds this to her weekly schedule. He also makes a note to send a photo and brief profile of Jennifer's work at the daycare to the collegiate webfeed on student contributions.

Geoff then asks Jennifer the most difficult question of their meeting: in what specific way is Jennifer challenging herself this year? As part of the overall ethic of the Collegiate, all students are encouraged to identify specific ways they intend to stretch themselves beyond the boundaries of their current abilities or comfort zones. This ends up being a very personal goal. For some students, it involves overcoming a fear of public speaking; for others, it means taking on a leadership role in a group or on a team; for others still, it might mean completing a difficult outdoor expedition or pushing oneself to the next level in musical ability.

This is a difficult question for Jennifer because she tends to play it safe. Her decision last year to explore the rougher part of her city was a big step. This year, she isn't sure what she wants to do. Geoff asks what she is most afraid of. After a few minutes of reflection, Jennifer answers, "Meeting new people." Geoff eventually convinces Jennifer to sign up for a completely new World Watch group with individuals she has not met before.

Geoff finishes off the meeting by reviewing Jennifer's progress on her Masterworks project. Because her committee has forwarded positive reports, Geoff is complimentary of Jennifer's progress. He reminds her, nonetheless, of upcoming due dates and encourages her to keep moving along.

Jennifer is out of her PA meeting by 4:30 and heads for home. She knows that she has to read 40 pages of Jane Austen and keep on track with all other elements of the program, but she is happy with how things are going. She is connected with a variety of peer groups through her lunch friends, Thursday badminton, book clubs, project advisors, and World Watch buddies. She is excited about completing her Masterworks project and figuring out an interesting culture shock exploration. She is nervous about joining a new World Watch club but has learned from experience that it might lead to other things.

Jennifer knows that, eventually, she will have to figure out what she wants to do with her life. In the meantime, she is enjoying becoming more competent and confident in her abilities, trying out new things, and gaining a big picture sense of her place in the world. She knows she is building a foundation to do something remarkable with her life, and she is excited to discover what that may be.

Pathways for Educators

I believe that grade school education needs to change. By aiming too low in our aspirations, we have created a pale approximation of what education could be. We did this in the industrial factory-school version of schooling, and we are in danger of doing so again by way of a potentially misguided emphasis on skills and a superficial understanding of personalized learning.

I also believe, however, that now is a time of great opportunity for teachers, educational leaders, and the community at large. We already have in our hands the ideas, resources, and technology to significantly transform our schools for the better. What's missing is a shared commitment to a richer version of education and a willingness on our part to make the architectural changes necessary to deliver on its most important purposes.

Teachers and educational leaders, working together, have to be at the epicenter of the changes to come. This will be no easy task, because it is difficult to let go of long-held assumptions. How our children will experience school, however, can be significantly *different*—and significantly *better*—than the way we experienced school. While there is cause for optimism in the commitment and energy of younger teachers, this must be balanced against the experience of committed educational leaders who understand the structural changes needed to unleash the full potential of schools.

What follows are a few suggestions about how teachers and educational leaders can approach the challenges ahead.

START WITH CLARITY OF PURPOSE

Start by asking "why" before "how." If you are a teacher, ask yourself why you got into the profession in the first place. What were you hoping to accomplish with your students? What sticks do you bring to the fire? If you are an educational leader, ask these things as well, but ask also how you think education in general—and then your school, in particular—is meant to contribute to the well-being of individual children and society as a whole. Make sure you aim deep and high enough in your aspirations.

CREATE TIME TO BREATHE, THINK, AND PLAN

Teachers and educational leaders alike can easily get completely caught up in the minutiae and enormity of their day-to-day responsibilities. If we want even half a chance to bring about the system changes introduced in this book, we are going to need to find some breathing space to imagine, plan, evaluate, and analyse the changes we think we want to make.

The first challenge is to make sure the educational leaders in the building actually get some time to breathe and think. I vividly recall how hard it was for me to hack my way out of the underbrush of budgets, parent communications, staff development, human resources adventures, building maintenance, and procurement to get a few moments to think about the program as a whole and determine what strategic initiatives we needed to pursue. I suspect that the situation is the same for most school leaders. Because we do not give ourselves the time to look at the big picture, we scurry about sustaining our schools as they are instead of making at least some structural moves to transform them into something even better. Every once in a while, we need to look at the broader horizon.

Finding thinking time as educational leaders, in particular, is easier said than done. Here are a couple of strategies that I have used or have seen used by colleagues:

Break up your "To Do" list into whatever categories make sense to you—e.g., admin, program, staff, students, parents, finance—but make sure you have a category called "Big Picture" or "Strategic Planning" that sits as a priority at the front of your categories. (Note that there should only be a maximum of 3-4 items listed in this category.)

Look at your planner and set aside a *consistent period of time* where you will address the items on that list. Find a time where it is least likely you would be required to attend to other matters, such as school events, parent meetings, and staff observations.

Don't be afraid to close your door. Let your administrative staff that know that the thinking time you have set aside for yourself is off limits, except in cases of emergency. (Define what you mean by emergencies, and delegate authority to others to deal with "mini-emergencies.")

Find a colleague—or perhaps a supervisor—with whom you can candidly discuss progress on your "Big Picture" or "Strategic Initiatives" list. Meet with them at least once every 3-4 weeks.

Use professional development conferences as an opportunity to think outside the normal parameters of your school. If you happen to be on a flight, use that time to ask "what if..." If you are in a presentation that sparks an idea, skip the next session and spend time in your hotel room figuring out how to translate that idea into a workable proposal for your own school.

There is a tendency among school leaders to concentrate most of our time on establishing and maintaining relationships with others—teachers, parents, and/or students because educational leadership is, after all, very much about managing people. But educational leadership is not just about managing people, it is also about understanding what we are trying to accomplish and why how best to proceed.

The second challenge is to find time for the staff as a whole to create or consider cross-school initiatives. These are not the kind of things that can be handled via staff bulletins or administrative meetings that only address day-to-day operations. As most educational leaders are aware, there needs to be, at the very least, a year-long process whereby new initiatives are introduced in the pre-planning sessions before the start of school, followed up on in monthly or bi-weekly workshops throughout the year, and then re-examined and evaluated in a full debrief at the end of the year. Ideally, in fact, ideas for improvements are collected throughout the previous year, perhaps by way of a shared document that is available to all the staff, with new initiatives then formally identified at the year-end debrief (where staff have an opportunity to discuss what worked and what didn't over the course of the year). These initiatives are then *reintroduced* in the pre-planning start-up sessions and implemented in conjunction with the monthly or bi-weekly monitoring workshops.

Schools are finding different ways to consistently schedule these all-important monitoring and development workshops. At IPS, we had an early dismissal (2:30) on Wednesday afternoons, which we used, in part, to schedule monthly staff workshops. Staff teaching schedules can be intentionally constructed to ensure that certain pods of people, such as department members or cross-grade cohorts, can meet together to address a relevant initiative. Some schools are also experimenting with weekly late-starts on a designated weekday to give multiple teams the opportunity to meet on a consistent basis.

All of this is, again, a matter of architecture—in this case, the architecture of time. The point for educational leaders and staff practitioners alike is that we can't leave strategic thinking and school improvement to the margins as something we will look at after we have completed all our "regular" duties, if at all. Strategic thinking and school improvement must become part of our regular duties. If we can create the time to make them so, we create the practical conditions that allow us to pursue our most important purposes.

FIND AN ENTRY POINT THAT WORKS FOR YOU

The changes anticipated in this book are significant and far-reaching. They also represent a very tangled ball of string; if you pull on one strand, others will be affected. If you decide to introduce an online component in one of your classes, you need to be ready with an alternative for the student who learns best by your direct intervention. If you radically reconfigure your instructional delivery timetable, you need to be prepared to reconstruct the job descriptions of your staff.

As most practitioners are aware, there is currently a debate in education that mirrors the focus of a broader conversation: the distinction between improvement and innovation[1]. The idea is that to improve a practice is to do what you already do, only more effectively; to innovate is to actually change what you do.

Innovation is all the rage right now—particularly "disruptive innovation"[2]. By now, we are familiar with the ways disruptive innovators such as Turbo Tax, VRBO, Uber, and Tangerine are capturing the clientele of traditional tax return outfits, hotels, taxi companies, and banks.

Clearly, much of what I am suggesting in this book amounts to innovation—perhaps even disruptive innovation. The end goal is clear: to fundamentally re-engineer schools to enable them to deliver on the true potential of education. The question is, how do we get to that endpoint?

The philosopher Otto Neurath once offered a beautiful metaphor when he compared the evolving nature of knowledge to a boat that must be repaired at sea: "We are like sailors who on the open sea must reconstruct their ship but are never able to start afresh from the bottom..."[3] This image has been used to describe the dilemma, and opportunity, of those who are attempting to make changes within an already-moving enterprise. The idea is that—absent the luxury of a drydock—teachers and educational leaders need to make changes one plank at a time.

My own sense is that we must do both things: rebuild our boats on the move and establish drydocks to create something new from the ground up. In existing schools, we can identify those one or two pivotal changes that will ultimately put us on the path to rethinking our entire way of doing things. At the provincial or state level, we can consider recreating laboratory schools connected to universities or special demonstration schools within districts.[4] In all cases, we would also be well served in further investigating more outlier schools (both public and independent) to find out what is promising and what is not.

The point is that, as teachers and educational leaders alike, we need to begin from an entry point that is realistic and doable within the context of our own particular situation. I would also underline, again, that we need to be at least a little impatient in our desire to make changes for the better. While we can't make expansive transformations overnight, we nonetheless need to maintain a quiet determination to move things along by being active and persistent agents for positive change.

COLLABORATE AND COLLUDE

It is now abundantly clear that for positive change to happen, educational leaders and teachers must work together. It will not be "top-down" directives or "bottom-up" movements that will win the day but instead a clearly-defined partnership between teachers and educational leaders that is directed toward a clearly-articulated common goal. Teachers and educational leaders each have distinctive contributions to make. Teachers must bring their ideas, commitment, and expertise to the table. Educational leaders must find a way to activate, situate, defend—and, if necessary, amend—those ideas in the larger context of the educational project as a whole and in the practical universe of what is achievable at a particular time. Teachers and educational leaders must feel like they are in this thing together and be prepared to back each other up when the going gets tough.

I used to love it when teachers would bring me both a problem *and* a proposed solution to the problem, as opposed to simply pointing out what was wrong and then expecting me to fix it. While I may not have been able to use their particular solution, or I needed to amend it, I recognized and appreciated them as a *participant* in our shared project rather than a mere bystander.

With this in mind, it is important that teachers and administrators never be afraid to "Ask Up" to their supervisor about new initiatives that they think could improve the learning situation for students. If you are a teacher or learning assistant with a great idea, run it by your principal. If you are a principal, book a meeting with your superintendent. If you are a superintendent who knows that things need to change, go to your state or provincial governing body. One school superintendent in British Columbia, for example, was dissatisfied with the provincial reporting structure, so he went to the Ministry of Education to ask for a change to the Ministerial Order on student assessment. He was able to get a temporary variance for his district to introduce a new, and ultimately successful, initiative. Changing education for the better is difficult and complex. We are going to need all the ideas we can get. If you have a good idea, put it on the table.

And finally, I have discovered—as both a teacher and an educational leader—that many of the most important insights come by way of conversations with colleagues in informal settings. Sometimes the ideas that begin on the back of a napkin are the ones that deserve to make it into the lives of our students.

SEEK OUT CONSTRUCTIVE PARTNERSHIPS

It really does take a village. Find those people in your community—sometimes parents, sometimes not—who might enjoy the opportunity to contribute in some way to the education of the young. The invitations can take many forms. Some examples:

- act as judges or enquiring audiences at school science fairs or art & design exhibitions
- serve as facilitators in parent-to-parent support groups
- be informed speakers in classes or at special event days
- contribute, as advisors, to Masterworks or Discovery Projects
- help run student book clubs
- coach after-school teams

Survey the educational programs that are already being offered in non-school organizations outside your building. Art galleries, planetariums, special produce farms, wildlife sanctuaries, and fish hatcheries almost always have some educational program associated with their work. One of our most popular school excursions was to the Vancouver Police Museum.

Find a way to connect with a university or college. We occasionally had university students run research projects at our school which yielded results that were of benefit to their work and informative for us. We also found ways to get our students to special college or university exhibits and presentations that were relevant to their general studies or projects.

It is also possible to get parents or local businesses involved in big projects. Our board chair, who was also a building contractor, was the driving force behind installing a special outdoor workshop and shed behind our school. He—along with a parent with experience in interior design—also helped us renovate our old library into a more user-friendly "Think Tank" for student collaboration and project work.

There is a wealth of external resources and goodwill out there to augment what we want to accomplish in schools. We just need to find them and ask.

COMMUNICATE

To make real change happen, we will need the active and committed support of parents and the community at large. Through one hundred years of professionalized schooling, our parents and citizens may have slipped into a complacent lethargy about the purpose and importance of education. In striving now to re-engineer our schools, we are also striving to reclaim education as a public good. Our job as teachers and educational leaders will be as much about equipping and inspiring the *parents* as it will be about doing the same for our students.

This includes making sure we communicate clearly with parents about our emerging plans—and reasons—for the changes we want to make in the education of their children. Ideally, we need to get some portion of the parent population involved in at least some part of the initial planning process—perhaps by way of an initial "Education Roundtable" that introduces a particular issue and then a follow-up survey. Once a particular action is ready to launch, this needs to be communicated to the parent body as a whole. We found that the parent orientation sessions at the beginning of the year were a good place to introduce new initiatives. Well-developed "Letters to Parents" can also be an effective way to explain upcoming changes. The point is that parents need to be informed and on board about new initiatives if we expect them to support what we are doing.

STRUCTURE FOR SUCCESS

In schools, we need—at the very least—to contain our failures. Entrepreneurs like to encourage us to "fail early and fail often," but unlike the process of creating new widgets, we can't completely fail with other people's children. (Perhaps this is one of the reasons that educational innovation is so difficult—we are rightfully worried about doing harm to those in our care.) There are ways, nonetheless, to mitigate against the potential downside of some of our new initiatives:

- *Do your homework.* Research other examples where a similar approach has been attempted and try to anticipate the challenges you might have to confront.
- *Make sure that the relevant staff are on board.* Include them in the planning process and make sure there is an opportunity to evaluate and debrief the initiative.

- *Begin with pilot programs.* "Test drive" a new program for a restricted period—or with a restricted group of students (or staff)—to see what you learn.
- *Communicate early and often.* As stressed above, make sure the affected parents understand both the content and rationale for the change. Give them a heads-up about where you are going, and let them know how it went.
- *Get your students on board.* Show them the courtesy of giving them good reasons for the changes you would like to make. Get their feedback as well on how they think things are going.
- *Where possible, design initiatives with multiple potential benefits.* That way, if your target benefit does not, in fact, emerge, there will be others that may come to the fore.
- *Be honest.* Don't sugarcoat results. Be transparent and objective in your analysis of the success and failure of your initiatives.

Our responsibility to "structure for success" is really a responsibility to introduce our new initiatives with intelligence and integrity and with an eye to the well-being of our students. This applies equally to the individual teacher who wants to try a different approach with a student as it does to the educational leader who must shepherd in a significant structural change within the school as a whole.

PAY ATTENTION TO THE FOREST *AND* THE TREES

The "trees" are the individual students who walk through the doors of our classroom or school every morning. Our first responsibility is to pay attention to them as individual human beings, each with distinctive fears, expectations, wants, and needs. If they have an unhappy look on their face, we need to find time to take them aside and ask them how they are doing. If they are struggling in a project or academic course, we have to find a way to get them the support they need. The value of our work as teachers and educational leaders ultimately depends on how well we respond to each individual student under our care.

The "forest" is the bigger picture of our classrooms and schools in the context of the educative project as a whole—and, indeed, of the educative project in the context of human well-being. If we are going to make changes to course content, program elements, or instructional schedules, we need to make sure these changes link back to a deeper and richer expression of our most fundamental purposes. If we are changing just for the sake of being "innovative," we need to reconsider our motives. We need to ask again what that "forest" is really all about.

Pathways for Parents

I wanted this book to introduce parents to a broad survey of educational issues and innovations, so you can become allies with those teachers and educational leaders who are trying to transform education for the better. While I do not expect you to take the lead in making the specific architectural changes at schools yourselves—the teachers and educational leaders are best placed to do that—my hope is that you will be able to find and use those strategic moments, both at home and at school, where your input and support will make all the difference in the world.

PARENTS AS PRIMARY EDUCATORS

In two important ways, parents are the primary educators of children. You have the earliest and most extensive exposure to your kids in those crucial years of initial development. And, by far, you have the most vested interest in their overall well-being. You have both the access and motivation, therefore, to create the best possible conditions for the learning and growth that will follow. While well-run schools can certainly have a meaningful influence on a person's life, it is the family that establishes the initial foundation.

It is important, then, that parents first identify their own "why before how" when it comes to the educational trajectory of their own kids. I have proposed that the essential purpose of K-12 grade school education[1] is to help "equip and inspire students to cultivate their humanity." By this, I have meant that grade schools should immerse students in the kinds of foundational knowledge, skills, dispositions, and experiences that will enable them to discover and develop their interests and abilities and express their best selves. I have suggested, further, that this version of schooling offers students the best *educational foundation* from which to pursue and realize any number of life goals.

Parents need to figure out for themselves, however, what "equipping and inspiring" and "cultivating humanity" might look like with regard to their own children. Is the goal simply a matter of instilling "good manners?" Is it more a desire that your children gain inner confidence, or fortitude, or a sense of common decency? How important is competence, intelligence, or creativity in your picture? What about treating others with respect and care? And what specific things are you going to do—what particular kinds of equipping and inspiring are you going to bring about—to help your children acquire the capacities and attributes you most want for them?

If parents are going to work in partnership with schools, they need to know what they are bringing to the table. Asking their own "why before how" is a good place to start.

HOW TO SUPPORT *AND IMPROVE* YOUR CHILD'S SCHOOL

I propose that we now have the capacity to make schools much more powerful, authentic, and worthwhile than they have ever been. All that is needed is steadfast clarity of purpose and the license to make the structural changes required to transform the system.

Parents can help with both of these things.

We can begin by signaling to educators (and elected officials) that we will no longer accept an inadequate and unremarkable rendering of the educative project—expressed either as the comfortable mediocrity of the status quo or the superficiality of misguided innovation for its own sake. We can demand, this time around, that we aim high, that we create the kind of education for our kids that seeks to discover and develop their unique strengths within the larger narrative of cultivating our humanity.

How can parents do this? Here are four suggestions:

ASK THE RIGHT QUESTIONS

Start by asking yourself the following questions about your child's school:

- *In what particular ways* is the school helping to equip our children to interpret and navigate the world?
- *In what particular ways* is the school helping our children to identify and develop their strengths and interests, and perhaps even their passion in life?
- *In what particular ways* is the school helping our children to understand that they are part of a larger human narrative which—within its triumphs and tragedies—still offers an invitation to express the very best of what it is to be a human being?

As a parent, start by asking yourself the fundamental questions listed above and seeing how confident you feel about the answers, based on your own current knowledge of your child's school. Then, think about finding the right opportunities to direct an appropriate version of these questions respectfully, but clearly, to the educational leaders and teachers at your school. The responses you get to these "big picture" questions will give you a better understanding of the school's underlying principles and philosophy (or lack thereof). They may also help you understand particular challenges the school might face in striving to deliver a richer type of education.

Most schools have some sort of an orientation process to introduce you to the school and the people who will be working with your kids. You can usually get a pretty good feel for tenor and quality of the school by noticing what sorts of things are emphasized during these orientations. For example, here are two versions of possible introductory remarks that might be made by the leader of your school.

Brookdale High:

I hope you all had a good summer and are now ready to have your children get back to the books.

We were thrilled that our students recorded among the city's highest average test scores on final exams last year, and we are looking forward to doing even better this year.

Your children should have all been assigned a homeroom by now and should also have been given timetables showing their various classes. If you have any questions about your child's schedule, please contact a counsellor.

Please be sure to remind your sons and daughters that it is important that they check into their homerooms each morning, so they can confirm their attendance.

Before I finish, I would like to remind you that it is the responsibility of parents and students alike to familiarize yourselves with the school's code of conduct as well as the guidelines regarding the use of school facilities and equipment, which are posted on the school website.

If you ever have any questions or concerns, please know that my door is always open, and you can drop by anytime for a chat.

Hilltop Collegiate:

As this is the first day of a brand-new year, I want to say a few words to you about what we hope to accomplish together.

Our purpose at Hilltop Collegiate is to help equip and inspire students to cultivate their humanity [or some such other guiding purpose]. That sounds like a pretty ambitious goal—and it is. Let me try to explain what this means in terms of some of the things your sons and daughters will actually be doing through the year.

It means that they will get a thorough grounding in core skills like basic mathematics, grammar and sentence structure, expository writing, the fundamentals of rhetoric, reading for comprehension, and an introduction to reasoning.

But it also means that they will be introduced to what we like to call "the great conversations of human inquiry," which will help them understand how the ideas they will explore fit into the big story of civilization.

It means that we will give them opportunities to pursue their own questions and projects, with a view to helping them discover and develop their particular interests, abilities, and passions.

It means that they will have experiences that take them out of their own social and cultural milieu so they can begin to see things from a different perspective.

It means that they will have the chance to make a positive contribution to the community that they live in.

In short, we expect their time here to be much more than just a way station enroute to university or some other pursuit. We hope, instead, that their time with us will make a lasting impact on the rest of their lives.

But, in order for any of that to happen, we need the support and commitment of parents to help us give your children an education that is worthy of their time. The road ahead will not be straight and narrow. There will be diversions, mistakes, and miscues along the way. When those occur, we would ask only that you come and see us and work through solutions in the context of our bigger, shared project. Working together, we can do great things for our kids.

Thanks for listening. I look forward to getting to know all of you better this year.

The items that educational leaders choose to highlight at events like these sometimes—but not always—reveal their true priorities. Parents need to determine whether or not these priorities match their own.

If the school orientation session proves unsatisfactory, you might find it more suitable to raise these "big picture" questions in a private one-on-one meeting with the school principal or a teacher. It might be part of a general conversation about the school, or it might bridge from a discussion about specific issues or challenges that your child faces to a consideration of the bigger educational principles that are at stake.

It is important to frame these questions in a respectful and non-threatening or accusatory manner that encourages a frank and constructive conversation, not a defensive response. Ideally, they can be the beginning of a two-way dialogue that gets you both beyond discussing just the day-to-day "how" of your child's education and into the underlying "why."

All of this presupposes, of course, that the educational leaders themselves understand the true purpose and potential of education. I once had a principal offer me a tour of his school in which he was proud to show off his variety of learning facilities: an art room, a shop, and a recording studio, for starters. When I asked him why he thought it was important that students be given this range of opportunities—and what, moreover, the underlying rationale for his program was as a whole—I thought I was giving him an open invitation to sketch out his vision of education. Instead, he was flustered; he had apparently never been asked the question. He mumbled that the important thing was that students be given choice as to what they pursue, but he couldn't say why. It was as if choice alone were an end in itself. We can, and should, expect more than this from the people who lead our schools.

BE AN ACTIVE PARTNER

The second way that parents can support schools in providing the best possible education for students is to be active partners in the project, where your time and talents permit. This can happen in two ways: in your interactions with teachers and support personnel regarding your own children and by way of your contributions to the community as a whole.

In recommending a strong partnership between parents and instructional providers at the school, I cannot help but suggest one important caveat: your interactions should be selective and strategic rather than multitudinous and all-consuming. Teachers are very busy people. I once explained to a group of parents that an elementary school teacher's job is somewhat like single-handedly running a highly-organized, five-hour birthday party for 20-

30 kids, five days a week. But this, of course, does not adequately capture it because elementary school teachers—and their middle and high school colleagues—are doing much more than running birthday parties; they are trying to deliver a general educational program that meets the individual needs of every student in their class.[2] My heartfelt request, therefore, is that you pick your time and topic carefully when communicating with teachers. Try to be proactive by giving them a heads-up about potential issues before they emerge, and try to come away with just one or two shared strategies for moving forward.

Quite apart from the specific interest and attention that you may put into supporting your own child's education, there are many other ways you can contribute to the improvement of the school community as a whole. Here are a few examples:

- Serve as a Board Member (if your school has a board structure) or on a Community Council (if your school uses some version of site-based management).
- Serve on a board sub-committee or an ad hoc committee in an area of interest or expertise (Finance? Risk management? Interior design for new learning spaces?).
- Serve as a member of the Head's or Principal's parent liaison group[3], if there is such a thing.
- Serve as an Advisory Committee member on a student project that could benefit from your interest or expertise.
- Help arrange apprentice experiences, if these are part of your school's program.
- Help arrange informative speaker presentations or volunteer to be a speaker yourself.
- Volunteer your expertise in art, drama, music, or film if these are offered at your school.
- Help coach and/or supervise school-sanctioned teams (at games and tournaments).
- Help supervise special excursions.
- Host "project" parties for collaborative groups that want extra time to complete their work.
- Participate in school fundraising events (contribute what you can; if not monetarily, help with the organization).

A few important caveats are in order here as well.

The first is that many of these initiatives should be pursued "by invitation" of the school, not the other way around. At the very least, they should emerge out of a well-constructed overall plan as opposed to being the result of a particular individual parent's pet peeve.

When I served as Head of Island Pacific School, I had a number of occasions where people would come to me with "great ideas" that they hoped and expected would be taken up quickly. One person suggested that we create a course on manners and proper table etiquette, while another wanted us to teach kids how to balance a checkbook and calculate mortgage interest. While both might arguably be good lessons in and of themselves, the issue was where they might fit within a total program—both philosophically and in actual time. The problem was that, in those cases where I could not take up an individual's proposal, they would invariably become disillusioned about what they thought the school was trying to accomplish. My other sincere request, therefore, would be for individuals with great ideas to recognize that these must somehow fit within an overall purpose and understand that not all of them can happen all the time.

Another of our greatest challenges—and opportunities—is to find a way to get more adults involved in the education of our young. I'm referring not only to parents but also to local neighbours, grandparents, college and university professors, trade and craft experts, and people in the arts and business communities. At Island Pacific School, we used the phrase "Community Faculty" to denote pretty much anyone who came into the school—special speakers, Masterworks advisors, art & dance instructors—to share their knowledge, interest, and expertise with the students. I think that there is a vast, untapped potential of "Community Faculty" out there who could inject some real vitality into what we do in schools. Parent contributions are a good place to start.

CHAMPION EDUCATIONAL INNOVATORS

A third important contribution that parents can make to the improvement of grade school education is to support and champion those teachers and educational leaders who are already out there creating deeper and richer educational experiences for your kids. All of them are trying, in various ways, to re-engineer their practices. Some are experimenting with different versions of blended learning, while others are trying to figure out ways to make more open and fluid timetables. Some schools are putting more of an emphasis on project-based learning; others are exploring the possibilities of cross-grade grouping and variable class sizes. Some educators are even taking a second look at student assessment practices. By heading into uncharted territory, all of them are taking risks. They are doing so nonetheless because they have seen the deficiencies of the status quo and have a burning passion to make things better for students. They need your endorsement and support.

They will need this most acutely, moreover, when things go wrong. To completely re-engineer our education system is a significant undertaking. There are going to be glitches. While some of the potential problems can be mitigated through careful implementation—by running limited pilots projects first, for example—there are still going to be some misfires.

To be supportive—rather than reactive—when these occur, parents might bear in mind three things. First, all of these innovations will be attempted on the basis of goodwill: the teachers and educational leaders who pursue them do so because they want an improvement in the learning experience for your kids. Second, children are more resilient than we sometimes give them credit for. What we may regard as a major upset in their educational lives might not register as significantly to them in the grand scheme of things. Finally, despite our possible fears and worries, there is no going back. Educational change needs to happen. Our greatest contribution as parents is to support and endorse our teachers and educational leaders when things go well and encourage them to learn from mistakes and move on when difficulties emerge.

HELP PUT EDUCATION ON THE POLITICAL AGENDA.

You are doubly invested in the success of the education system—not only as a parent but also as a taxpayer. And, as a taxpayer and voter, there is the potential to be an agent for educational change at a political level as well at your local school.

Most voters would likely endorse the idea that education could be one of the most important factors in determining the shape and priorities of our society. Yet how often is the quality of public education identified as a key topic of political debate in the same way as health care, immigration, energy policy, or any other number of public policy issues? The reason, in part, is likely that the educational status quo still maintains a tremendous inertia. Chances are that most politicians are not currently hearing a lot from their constituents about an urgent need to raise the bar on public education. While they may utter the occasional platitudes about the vital importance of having good schools, the truth is that grade-school education does not usually register strongly on their political radars.

Of course, that can change if enough voters decide that public education really is a priority—that this huge investment we make in our children can, and should, be directed to more worthwhile purposes.

Some would say that looking to the political process for real improvement in the educational system would be a long game, with very long odds. Nonetheless, it strikes me as a game worth playing. It includes but also goes beyond advancing the immediate interests of our children to advancing the broader interests of society at large. We have bequeathed our future generations some enormously difficult challenges; therefore, we also need to bequeath them the best educational opportunities we possibly can in order to find solutions to those challenges and prosper as a society and a species.

WHAT CAN I DO AT HOME?

This book is not about "parenting" in the regular sense of how to raise your children. It is, however, about educating kids. Insofar as parents are the primary—and most important—educators of children, there are a few things that we can do outside of school and in our homes to support and complement what can and should be happening in good schools.

Many of these things are frankly obvious, and it is likely that you are already doing some or all of them. If so, good for you! If you are like me as a parent, however, you might sometimes be well-intentioned in thought but not always great on follow-through. The ideas presented below are therefore probably best read as gentle reminders for us to do what we already know is good for our children. Perhaps the new motivation here is to see them as essential contributing elements to that larger project of equipping and inspiring our kids to cultivate their humanity.

READ TO YOUR KIDS.

I made reference earlier in the book to the idea of "emancipatory competencies"—in other words, the kinds of abilities that, in fact, "free" a person to further extend their learning and growth. Having the interest and ability to read is, of course, one of the most fundamental emancipatory abilities a person can have. While it is true that most schools will eventually teach your child to read, we do our kids a huge service by introducing and habituating them to the written word early. It is not only capability that we want to cultivate but genuine interest—and a child's interest is partially determined by their success in mastering the form.

One of the best ways to introduce children to the written word is to read to them. Often. The most recent *Scholastic Kids and Family Reading Report*[4] has a number of interesting findings about the value and importance of reading at home:

- They define a "frequent reader" as someone who reads books for fun five or more times a week. (Infrequent readers read less than one day a week.)
- The three main factors in predicting if a child will become a frequent reader are that he enjoys reading, his parents are frequent readers, and he strongly believes that reading books for fun is important. (p. 2, 23)
- Overall, frequent readers are less likely than are infrequent readers to engage in common screen-related activities 5–7 days a week. (p. 26)
- The top reason children say they enjoy being read aloud to is that it's a special time with their parents. (p. 35)
- 40% of kids ages 6 to 11 whose parents have stopped reading aloud to them say they wish their parents had continued. (p.2)
- While 73% of parents with children ages 0 to 5 say they started reading aloud to their children before age one, only 30% say they began before the age of 3 months. (p. 2-3)
- The American Academy of Pediatrics recommends that parents read aloud to children starting at birth. (p. 3)

Despite these findings, there is growing evidence to show that parents are reading to their children less often. The Scholastic report, released in 2015, indicated that "children are reading somewhat less often than they did four years ago,"[5] while a more recent (2018) Nielsen Book Research survey from the UK reported that "while 69% of preschool children were read to daily in 2013, that figure had dropped to just 51%". Some of the reasons cited for that decline include "the struggle to find energy at the end of the day" and "the child's preference to do other things." The report also proposes that giving children the "freedom to pick their own reading material is far more effective in creating lifelong readers than a strict reading list".[6]

The advantage of an old-fashioned bedtime story (with a book) is that it serves a number of purposes simultaneously. It presents a story but also opens the door to the world of the written word. It strengthens and broadens imaginative capacity. It provides a time of quiet intimacy between you and your child at the end of every day. It is a soothing, predictable ritual that makes bedtime something to look forward to and will help your child get to sleep.

Short picture books with simple words offer a particularly good introduction to reading. Longer volumes provide the opportunity to tell more interesting stories. Parents should be reading both of these: the first to experiment with simple words, and the second to invite and entice their children toward the possibilities that await them.

A side benefit is the opportunity to read some wonderful books you might otherwise never encounter. A friend recalls a regular bedtime reading routine that allowed him and his son to share C.S. Lewis' *Narnia* series, Tolkien's *Lord of the Rings*, all the works of Roald Dahl, *Huckleberry Finn*, *The Yearling*, and countless picture books and other works of children's fiction. He remembers it as one of the most pleasurable experiences of early fatherhood.

EXPOSE YOUR CHILDREN TO NEW PEOPLE, PLACES, AND IDEAS

If one of the endgames of grade school education is to enable our kids to discover and further develop their particular interests and strengths, then we, as parents, need to help make that discovery process as broad as it can be. We have all heard stories of the kid who first discovered her passion at a museum, or a dirt-bike repair shop, or an art gallery, or a model rocket launch day, or a nature walk through the forest, or a dance recital, or a baseball game, or any number of other places. Part of our job as parents is to expose our children to as many potentially interesting experiences as we can in the knowledge that we are putting in front of them a parade of possible futures, one of which might eventually come home to roost.

In addition to arranging a multitude of mini-excursions, there is another way to do this. Be intentional about the people you invite into your home for dinner or a visit, and use the occasion to expose their story and ideas to your children. This takes a little doing because, first, you need to create a home environment where it makes sense for your children to observe and participate in adult conversations, and second, you need to show your children how to draw out the interesting and informative nuggets within a person's story through the asking of intelligent questions.

Everyone has a story, and within that story, there are always nuggets with the potential to inform or delight. The trick is to find a way to get beyond the obvious and mundane conversations we so often have—about the weather, for example—and extract the nuggets. You likely already know how to do this, so it is well worth teaching your children. You can show them that the trick is to ask your visitor a series of obvious, but nonetheless intelligent, questions that might include the following:

- What do you do (or what project are you currently working on)?
- What is the most difficult thing about your work (or the project you are currently working on)?
- What is the most interesting or rewarding thing about your work (or the project you are currently working on)?

The intelligent questions that necessarily follow will include some combination of "Why do you think that?", "How does that work?" and "Can you give me an example of what that looks like?"

Another less career-focused way of starting that might be asked of a friend rather than a stranger might be to enquire, "What thing currently has you most fascinated or vexed at the moment?" In either case, if you lead with the starter questions and then probe with relevant follow-up interrogatives, you can be guaranteed of learning something new and perhaps even become delighted by what you learn. Most importantly, if you model these conversations for your children—and then invite them to ask their own questions along the way—you will not only expose them to a rich variety of stories but also teach them how to open doors for innumerable possible futures.

To those who would say that young people are incapable of this kind of discourse, I would propose the opposite. I have found that if you honour and respect the potential intelligence of young people—and even intentionally raise the bar a little above their apparent capacity—they will strive mightily to make the jump.

That said, some of these attempts to broaden the experiences of our kids will undoubtedly fall flat. Some of the mini-excursions will elicit blank faces, and some of our most meticulously planned discussions will not go anywhere. My parents tried to introduce me to baseball, but it never caught on for me. That's okay. Part of the object here is for your child to also figure out where they have limited interest or ability (provided, of course, that they give everything their best shot). The point is not to prematurely direct our kids down particular paths but instead to expose them to the wide variety of possibilities that are out there.

SEEK OUT OPPORTUNITIES TO ACKNOWLEDGE YOUR CHILDREN'S EFFORT, INSIGHT, AND INTEGRITY

Most parents are likely pretty good at praising their children when they have done something well in terms of an overt ability, for example hit a home run or drawn a nice picture. Maybe this comes naturally to most of us. We might be a little less forthcoming, however, when it comes to acknowledging and supporting their emerging expressions of character. While we might be proud of our kids in our hearts, we might assume that their tentative explorations toward virtue should be quietly observed from afar.

We need to avoid this assumption. Nothing is more powerful for a person than to be acknowledged for doing the right thing by someone they love and respect. It takes a thousand tiny gestures and words of encouragement to help cultivate a defining attribute of one's character. Comments like "You are really working hard at this," "That was very perceptive" and "You showed a lot of integrity by doing the right thing here" are the shots in the arm that our kids need—indeed, that we all need—to help us head in the right direction. Parents are in the best position to do this.

Mind you, it has to be done well. It can't be fake, and it can't be done so often that children come to believe that their parents think they walk on water. Sometimes, in fact, parents need to call their kids on their lack of effort, perceptiveness, or integrity. As most of you already know, we need to take care to frame this not as an accusation which assumes a permanent character flaw but instead as an invitation to overcome a temporary slip from what you know to be their better selves. I have found—with both students and adults alike, by the way—that if you create the expectation for them to express their better selves, they almost always accept the invitation.

Your feedback—laudatory or corrective—should always be done one-to-one, preferably in a quiet place where you have a chance to look your young one in the eye. Helping your kids to create a strong foundation for who they are going to be in the world is one of the most important things you can do for them.

LET YOUR KIDS KNOW THAT THEY CAN BE GOOD AT THINGS THEY THOUGHT THEY COULD NOT BE GOOD AT

I have seen it time and time again at school. The kid who shows an initial interest in something then becomes quickly defeated because she has convinced herself that she is "just not good" at whatever they are undertaking. The truth is that most people can become reasonably good at something if they put in the hours (and take the advice and support that is given to them). Sure, there will always be that small percentage of people who are "naturally" gifted in particular areas, but for the vast majority of us, gaining competence in something is really just a matter of concentrated effort. Athletes and musicians already know this. They have learned that hard work—and good advice and support from coaches and mentors—is the key to eventual mastery. The lesson you impart to your child, therefore, is that when it comes to learning something new, success is less about "smarts" and more about tenacity.

GIVE YOUR KIDS SPACE…AND REASONABLE BOUNDARIES

One of the biggest challenges of parenthood is to figure out when to hold your kids close and when to give them breathing room. We needed to figure this out in the context of our middle school, and it is something that parents have to figure out, writ large, in the context of their kid's entire lives. It is an educational life lesson we are both responsible for.

Most of us are now familiar with the "helicopter parents" who are completely overbearing when it comes to the lives of their children. These are the parents who finish their children's sentences, always want special considerations that are unrelated to their child's actual needs and have very definite ideas about the optimum trajectory of their child's future.

I will never forget the brief side conversation I had with a student guide when I was visiting a very prestigious independent school. She explained that this was a school where students were meant to follow very deliberate paths to "success," which, for her own parents in particular, meant getting good grades so she could attend business school. Her heart, however, was in music and art. In the two-minute conversation I had with her, I realized that hers was a life destined for disappointment and profound unhappiness.

When we control the lives of our children too much, we rob them of one of the most important gifts of being human: the ability to determine at least some part of our lives for ourselves. Sometimes, in our understandable desire to "protect" our children, we actually diminish them.

On the other end of the spectrum are those parents who have almost no connection to their children whatsoever. These are the parents who are content to allow their offspring to pick up their "life lessons" from any source and be subject to whatever consequences naturally follow. Theirs are what are sometimes called the "free range" children—or the children "raised by wolves"—who have little experience in dealing with the normal constraints and conventions of human life and who, therefore, encounter more trouble than they need to.

I can always spot a "free range kid." They are the ones who say that their parents don't care how long they stay out or what extracurricular activities they engage in. While their words proclaim the extent of their freedom, the tone of voice is almost always bitter and dismissive: they actually want their parents to care.

Parents who take this "free range" approach might do so for a variety of reasons. They might have a strong philosophical commitment to the indiscriminate value of unfettered freedom. They might be psychologically uncomfortable about imposing their values on their children. They might be overwhelmed by work and simply not have the time to attend to their children. Or they might not, in fact, be very interested in the lives of their children. To these parents, I would say that we should never underestimate the crucial importance of the direction, care, and attention that we bestow upon our children, particularly in their formative years. While their lives are indeed their own, they nonetheless look to us as their initial referent to make sense of the world.

This tension between guiding children and giving them breathing space is indeed a tricky one. While it becomes particularly obvious in the middle years when kids have one foot in their family circle and the other in the orbit of their friends, it also extends into high school and beyond. In striving to increase our children's sense of agency and responsibility as they mature, we should expect them to demand some measure of independence. The challenge is to figure out what kind of independence in what context.

As a parent, you have probably already realized the importance of allowing "freedom within boundaries" for your children. The basic idea is simple: there are inviolable ground rules that can't be broken without invoking serious consequences (the boundaries), and there are freedoms that can be exercised within those boundaries—although these too can be subject to operational protocols.

To take a simple example, at Island Pacific School we specified the actual physical property boundaries beyond which the students could not go. Within those boundaries, our general operational parameter to the students was that they should "use their heads" to determine which behaviours and activities could be reasonably defended, and which could not. They had free access at lunch to dishes, cutlery, and microwaves as well as all the instructional spaces in the building. They also played outside on the back field, the parking lot, and down by the creek. This, by and large, worked remarkably well. While there were a few minor mishaps along the way and a couple of times where we had to clarify to our middle school students what "using their heads" required in particular circumstances, the overriding benefit was to create an environment where students could exercise their independence within an understood framework of reasonable constraints.

Some clear boundaries (or ground rules) that parents might impose on their younger children might include not hitting their younger brother or not having a tantrum when they want something. The consequence here could be immediate removal to the child's room, followed later by an apology to the little brother. Ground rules for older offspring could be, "Don't drink and drive" or "Be home by midnight." Some operational parameters within those boundaries might include: "Don't do anything that would endanger your life or the lives of others" or "Let me know, at all times, where you are."

When the ground rules are broken, the consequences need to be immediate and commensurate with the severity of the infraction. There should not be a lot of conversation here. As long as the ground rules and the consequences were clearly understood, the administration of the consequences—e.g., you are grounded for two weekends—should be pretty straightforward. This is also not a time that you want to get mad and yell at your child. (Remember, we all make mistakes, so we should expect this kind of thing.) Instead, it is a time to underline that bad decisions do indeed have consequences. And, finally, this is not a time to renegotiate or amend the ground rules. That conversation can come after; consequences come first.

The point is that we need to define different kinds of boundaries and operational parameters for different kids at different times. Most importantly, we also need to intentionally create appropriate open spaces as our kids mature.

CONNECT WITH OTHERS

Parenting in the 21st century is a difficult proposition—particularly parenting with an intention to meaningfully support your child's overall education. The external messages that our children are exposed to through internet sites and social media can easily usurp the narratives of parents and teachers. While tweens and teens spend about 1,000 hours of their year in schools, they average another 1,925 hours per year on entertainment media use.[7] In addition to the very real life challenges that parents have to face—anxiety, anorexia, depression, suicide—there are also the regular ups and downs their children need to navigate: discovering their strengths and challenges, learning to get along with others, etc.

One of the best things that parents can do to help their kids—and themselves—survive and thrive within the school years is to create consistent opportunities to speak with one another about the joys and frustrations of raising children. The advice of so-called "experts" (including myself) needs to be tempered with the experience of actual parents in the thick of things.

It took me awhile to figure this out. In the year before I retired from Island Pacific School, I encouraged two parents with professional training in parenting and counseling to consider running informal discussion groups to share ideas, strategies, and stories. This turned out to be one of the most important resources for the parents who got involved. Just taking the time to share their fears, challenges, breakthroughs, and setbacks made all the difference in the world. While the parent facilitators offered a few suggested strategies, it was always up to the individual to determine how best to incorporate these in the context of their own family situation. The idea has apparently caught on; they now hold regular sessions with a much larger number of participants.

TEACH *OUR* CHILDREN WELL

I take it as given that one of the most important—and sometimes most difficult—elements within a child's overall education is the cultivation of their integrity and moral sensibility. Here, especially, is where the family must lay a strong foundation. While schools must certainly endorse and operationalize the principle of respect for persons, it rests with the family to introduce basic moral precepts to their children and then support and sustain these as they mature.

On one level, this is relatively easy to do. Parents can introduce their young children to the basic ideas that lying, cheating, stealing, and treating people badly, for example, are wrong and shouldn't be done. The challenge comes, of course, when they break one or more of these precepts. Again, it is not so much a matter of creating the conditions to ensure that children will never do anything wrong (which is unrealistic and possibly unhealthy) as it is about creating environments—including a home environment—to deal with the inevitable transgressions. If you can assure your child that "We all make mistakes" but then also require that they take responsibility for their actions, attempt to make amends, and deal forthrightly with the consequences, you will put them in a strong position to learn from their experience and move on.

While these little object lessons in life will sometimes be uncomfortable, they are nonetheless necessary. More importantly, they are not the kinds of lessons that can be left to the default culture of our time because that culture is notoriously ambiguous on so many issues of who is responsible for what. Here again, the onus—and the privilege—of helping young people navigate the moral challenges of life begins at home.

Conclusion

The Heart of the Matter: Happiness

When I ask parents what they want most for their kids at school, almost all of them say, "I just want them to be happy." When I probe as to what they mean by this, they usually offer some combination of the following:

- to feel safe and secure
- to have fun
- to make good friends
- to feel that they are being listened to and have something worthwhile to contribute
- to have the opportunity to discover and demonstrate their own strengths
- to feel justifiably confident in their knowledge and abilities in at least some areas
- to be passionately interested in something
- to be healthy
- to be loved and recognized for who they are

When I ask teachers and educational leaders what they most want for their students, they too end up saying more or less the same thing:

- to feel good about attending school and be confident that they will be supported academically, socially, and emotionally

- to be alive; to be able to have fun and be silly
- to be willing to embrace challenges and enjoy them
- to feel that they have value—something to contribute
- to have their curiosity piqued
- to realise the incredible power they have to shape not only their own future but also to have a significant impact in the world
- to feel a sense of worth in the world (vs feeling helpless or even disengaged)
- to be compassionate toward all beings

It seems to me that one of our own teachers summed it up perfectly when he said:

> *"Happiness. That's what I want for my students. While of course that is couched in many other things, at the end of the day it all boils down to happiness."*

This teacher is right to observe that happiness is couched "in many other things." There are at least two overlapping versions of happiness that are being expressed here by parents and educators alike. One is the happiness of safety, security, and self-confidence; the other is the happiness of human fulfilment.

The first is self-explanatory, while the second was best captured by Aristotle. He said that happiness is an end in itself and is expressed by the extent to which one has lived up to their full potential as a human being. This is not the happiness of instant gratification. It is instead the deeper happiness that includes health, friendship, love, and the fulfilment of discovering and developing our abilities, interests, and passions in the context of a larger narrative about a life well-lived. Parents and educators who have focused on the goal of cultivating human happiness are clearly onto something.

THE SCHOOLS OUR CHILDREN NEED

So, how do we create schools that enable—rather than act against—this double formulation of happiness?

First, and most obviously, we need to make sure that students feel safe, secure, and supported in our schools. If students come into our buildings with a bad feeling in their stomachs, we are doing something wrong. This is not to say that we should never challenge students, for indeed we should. It is only to say that we must make sure that our students are properly supported in the challenges we give them.

Second—and most importantly—we need to embrace foundational purposes that are worthy of our students and our society as a whole. It is a pale approximation of education to simply run students through an endless series of assignments and requirements to measure their apparent understanding or competency, so we can then produce transcripts to certify how far along they got on each descriptor. We must aim higher than that. We need to see that our job—as parents and educators alike—is to help equip and inspire our kids to cultivate their humanity. We need to give them the support, encouragement, and tools to discover their calling and to express the very best of who they are.

We must try our best to do many other things as well:

- eliminate those pernicious elements of the dominant model, while at the same time being careful that we do not replace it with something equally superficial
- make sure we do not allow the pursuit of skills to supercede the exploration of knowledge
- pay close and precise attention to the way in which structure (time, space, and number) either enables or incapacitates learning and engagement—to see that reconfigured structural arrangements are at the heart of a deeper, richer, better education for our young
- acknowledge the vast diversity of our students' interests and abilities and build in support systems to enable each and every one of them to find their path
- embrace the profound potential of technology, *properly used*, to significantly transform the educational experience of our students; see that we have a new lever here that can help us deliver on a quality education for all

- reconstitute the aims of our student assessment system and build an appropriate mechanism to reflect those purposes
- make a strong case why education—public education in particular—should receive strong financial support and be willing to explore different funding mechanisms to sustain our schools
- learn what we can from outlier schools, all the while being mindful about which elements we can realistically adopt within our own circumstances
- find a way to encourage and support broader leadership responsibilities on the part of the administrators who operate our schools
- find the right balance in the way we introduce and emphasize the "baseline, application, and extension" elements of learning
- make sure we do the right thing at the right time with a view, in particular, to building capacity for student agency
- invite teachers—and curriculum designers, workshops leaders, paraprofessionals, and community mentors—to become educators by reconnecting them to the larger purposes of education and showing them the contribution *they* make to something that is eminently worthwhile
- understand why "school culture matters"—why a climate of expectation, acknowledgement, and celebration is the fertile ground where genuine education can take root

And, we need to teach our children well. We have to show them how to be decent human beings, and we need to redirect them when they are not.

OUR BEST HOPE

This project of re-imagining the purpose of education and then re-engineering our schools to deliver on that purpose is a significant undertaking. Our best hope in accomplishing all of this is to forge a strong partnership between informed parents and those educators—upcoming and experienced—who are passionate about giving all students the kind of education that is worthy of the name.

This will work best with parents who take responsibility for themselves as the primary educators of their children—parents who read to the kids, expose them to new ideas, acknowledge their triumphs, give them appropriate space and boundaries, and help them navigate the moral challenges of life. It also requires parents who are willing to actively support improvement and innovation in schools by asking good questions, volunteering to help, supporting promising initiatives, and actively endorsing strong financial support for education.

In partnership with these parents, we must support those teachers and educational leaders with the courage and capacity to make the changes that need to happen to transform our schools for the better. We need to give them the license and support to work out the best possible learning configurations for students in a way that will complement and enable our larger purposes.

A CHALLENGE AND AN OPPORTUNITY

It seems to me that we are currently in danger of creating a world where self-interest progressively overtakes collective well-being and indeed any sense of humanity at all.

We see it where older citizens are unwilling to devote their tax dollars to school funding spent on "other people's kids." We see it when the talk show listener asks, "How is that *my* problem?" when someone cannot find a place to live. And we see it when governments make decisions on the basis of political posturing at the cost of our basic humanity.

All of this is a surrender of the idea that a society, acting together, can and should uphold a standard of care that goes beyond mere self-interest. It is a descent, instead, into a narrow and pitiful world.

We have an opportunity, however, to help steer the ship in a different direction.

If we were to take seriously that our job as educators—and indeed as parents and citizens—is to equip and inspire young people to cultivate their humanity, and to then fashion our schools accordingly, we would begin the process of creating a better world for ourselves and the next generation. If we could become committed to pursuing the *deep* prosperity of individuals coming to discover the unique gifts they can contribute to others, we would set ourselves up to realize goods that are greater than the sum of our parts.

We already have the ideas, resources, and technology at our fingertips to transform schools. We just need to commit to a deeper vision of education and have the courage to follow through on what we already know matters most.

We have the option, in other words, of choosing love.

Chapter Notes

Challenges and Opportunities

1. BC Ministry of Education.
http://www.bced.gov.bc.ca/reports/pdfs/sat_survey/public.pdf, p. 8

2. Michael Fullan, *Three Ways to Drive System Wide Change*,
https://www.youtube.com/watch?v=tws8N4c3eAA, May 14, 2015. Accessed: Dec13, 2017. See also: Michael Fullan and Maria Langworthy, *Towards a New End: New Pedagogies for Deep Learning*. Seattle: Collaborative Impact, June, 2013. p.1.

3. BC Ministry of Education.
http://www.bced.gov.bc.ca/reports/pdfs/sat_survey/public.pdf, p. 10

4. *BC Leading rise in private school enrolment across Canada*. CBC News, June 27, 2017; *Private School Enrolment,* National Center for Educational Statistics, updated January, 2018.
https://nces.ed.gov/programs/coe/indicator_cgc.asp

5. Michael Leachman, Kathleen Masterson, Eric Figueroa, *A Punishing Decade for School Funding*, Center on Budget and Policy Priorities, Report:November 29,2017, https://www.cbpp.org/research/state-budget-and-tax/a-punishing-decade-for-school-funding

What Possessed Me?

1. In the 1970s a student named Markus Janisch died of a pre-existing brain aneurysm during an inter-school snowshoe race. On June 12, 1979, twelve

students and a staff member lost their lives in a canoeing disaster on Lake Timiskaming in Ontario.

2. In 2000, Kenneth Mealey pleaded guilty to five counts of sexual assault while working at St. John's in Manitoba during the 1982-83 academic year. http://www.cbc.ca/news/canada/guilty-plea-on-sex-assault-charges-1.210991

Lesson #1: Why Before How

1. In 1952, University Chicago president Robert Maynard Hutchins and Mortimer Adler released a 54 volume compendium entitled Great Books of the Western World, published by Encyclopedia Britannica. The first volume, entitled The Great Conversation, was a discourse on liberal education. In 1963, Britannica published Gateway to the Great Books to introduce readers to the authors and ideas in the original set. There is now a Great Books Foundation that offers K-12 readings and support material through an online website. (www.greatbooks.org)

2. Hirsch, E.D., *Cultural Literacy: What Every American Needs to Know*, New York: Vintage Books, 1988.

3. Bennett, William J.; Finn, Chester E.; Cribb, John T., *The Educated Child: A Parent's Guide from Preschool through Eighth Grade.* New York: The Free Press, 1999.

4. "A child is innately wise and realistic. If left to himself without adult suggestion of any kind, he will develop as far as he is capable of developing." A. S. Neill. See also: A.S. Neill, *Summerhill: A Radical Approach to Child Rearing*, Hart Publishing, New York, 1960.

5. Educational leaders have managed this in this in different ways. Bob Snowden, a venerable Head of St. Michaels University School in Victoria, British Columbia, wrote a series of blogs on various educational topics that were linked together by a core philosophical thread. For another example, see Appendix 3, where you will find a short summation of remarks I made at a school orientation at the beginning of my final year at Island Pacific School.

Lesson #2: Matching Program to Purpose

1. I am wholly indebted to Dr. LeRoi Daniels and Dr. Jerrold Coombs, and Carol LaBar for their tremendous work on practical reasoning through the Association for Values Education Research (AVER) at the University of British Columbia.

2. While ethical theory, to be sure, can be more complicated than this, the basic idea here is to illuminate the implicit premises within arguments and then consider their defensibility and their relationship to one another.

3. Isaac Asimov, Column in *Newsweek* (21 January 1980)

4. See Appendix 2 for a more complete list of Masterworks titles that have been presented at Island Pacific School.

From the Dominant to the Ascendant Model of Schooling

1. Another version of this quote reads as follows: *"Our schools are, in a sense, factories, in which the raw products (children) are to be shaped and fashioned into products to meet the various demands of life. The specifications for manufacturing come from the demands of twentieth-century civilization, and it is the business of the school to build its pupils according to the specifications laid down."*

2. Todd Rose, *The End of Average; How We Succeed in a World That Values Sameness*. (Toronto; Harper Collins, 2016) 50.

3. John Taylor Gatto, *The Underground History of American Education*, (Odysseus Group, 2001), 222. Quoted in Todd Rose, *The End of Average; How We Succeed in a World That Values Sameness*. (Toronto; Harper Collins, 2016) 51.

4. Todd Rose, Ibid, p. 53

5. Todd Rose, Ibid, p. 54

6. Todd Rose, Ibid, p. 53

7. Jonich, The State Positivist, 21-22. Paraphrased from *The End of Average; How We Succeed in a World That Values Sameness*. (Toronto: Harper Collins,

2016) 53.

8. See, for example: A.S. Neill, *Summerhill: A Radical Approach to Child Rearing* (1960); Paul Goodman, *Compulsory Mis-Education and the Community of Scholars* (1962); Neil Postman & Charles Weingartner, *Teaching as a Subversive Activity* (1969); Ivan Illich, *Deschooling Society* (1970); Charles Silberman, *Crisis in the Classroom: The Remaking of American Education* (1970).

9. For a reasonably good explanation of many examples of educational jargon, see the Glossary of Educational Reform at: https://www.edglossary.org/

10. http://choiceschool.org/about-us/what-makes-choice-school-unique/. The School has, in fact, evolved over the years where it initially emphasized this capacity for free choice, but now positions itself more as a special education school for the Gifted.

11. http://www.selfdesign.com/story.html

12. The precursor to personalized learning is a practice known as "differentiated instruction". The basic idea is that teachers need to differentiate their instruction to best suit the particular needs of their individual students. The emphasis here was not so much on using technology to differentiate, but instead of being cognizant of the different learning modalities of students—oral, visual, auditory—and adjusting instruction accordingly.

13. Michael B. Horn & Heather Staker, Blended: Using Disruptive Innovation to Improve Schools, Jossey-Bass, 2015. p. 9-11

14. Education 2020
www.education-2020.wikispaces.com/21st+Century+Learning (March 2016)

15. Partnership for 21st Century Skills www.p21.org (March 2016)

16. Note that while the Partnership for 21st Century Learning Skills allows that students should also learn "core subjects", which include the "3R's and 21st Century Learning Themes", it is clear by their framework that it is the identified skills that are meant to comprise the majority of the curriculum. Skills, not knowledge, are becoming the primary content of contemporary schooling.

17. See Robin Barrow, *Understanding Skills: Thinking, Feeling and Caring*, London, Ontario: Althouse Press, 1990

18. In 1974, the British educational philosopher Paul Hirst published a remarkable paper entitled *Liberal Education and the Nature of Knowledge* in which he proposed that there are distinct "forms of knowledge" each having their own distinct concepts, logical structure, tests against experience, and techniques and skills. It follows that in order to "think critically" within any particular form of knowledge, one first has to have a thorough understanding of the basic architecture of that particular way of seeing. Put differently, the language of literary analysis is different than the language of physics, and in order to "think critically" about either of these, one first has to master the language.

The moral philosopher Alasdair MacIntyre came at this in a different way. He proposed that there are standards which define what he called practices (e.g., architecture, physics, etc.), and that in order to get *on the inside of a practice* one has to become intimately familiar with those practices. (See, MacIntyre, *After Virtue*, University of Notre Dame Press, 2nd Edition, 1984. p.187-191)

19. Ivan Illich, et. al., *After Deschooling, What?*, New York: Harper and Row, 1973.

The Heart of the Matter: Why Before How

1. Martha Nussbaum, *Cultivating Humanity*, Cambridge: Harvard University Press, 1997.

2. Charles Bailey, *Beyond the Present and Particular*, London: Routledge & Kegan Paul, 1894.

Structure Matters: Bring in the Architects

1. Hill, Alex; Mellon, Liz; Laker, Ben; Goddard, Jules, *The One Type of Leader Who Can Turn Around a Failing School*, Harvard Business Review, October, 2017; Updated March 3, 2017

2. Ibid.

3. Ibid.

4. Ibid.

5. Ken Robinson, *How To Change Education - From the Ground Up.* https://www.youtube.com/watch?v=BEsZOnyQzxQ

Structure Matters: Back to the Drawing Board

1. https://www.louvre.fr/en/visites-en-ligne

2.https://www.pbslearningmedia.org/resource/phy03.sci.phys.matter.ptabl e/periodic-table-of-the-elements/?#.Wot5kxPwaNY

3. http://froggy.lbl.gov/cgi-bin/dissect?engl

4. https://spacemath.gsfc.nasa.gov/media.html

5. To access a good number of teacher-curated digital resources (with live links) that were reviewed in a Blended Learning Pilot program at Island Pacific School, use this link: https://docs.google.com/document/d/1XVxVT7pAwfnbzFvFWizWfdZBms2x 2IGsOG16HxvpWg0/edit?usp=sharing

6. Michael B. Horn & Heather Staker, Blended: Using Disruptive Innovation to Improve Schools, San Francisco: Jossey-Bass (Wiley Brand), 2015.

7. Ibid, p. 53

8. Ibid, p. 37-51

9. http://www.rsed.org/index.cfm

10. https://www.altschool.com/

11. http://www.actonacademy.org/

12. http://www.globalonlineacademy.org/

13. https://www.connectionsacademy.com/

14. Michael B. Horn & Heather Staker, Blended: Using Disruptive Innovation to Improve Schools, Jossey-Bass (Wiley Brand): San Francisco, 2015. p. 36, 53

15. Glossary of Educational Reform, "Carnegie Unit", (updated 08.29.13), https://www.edglossary.org/carnegie-unit/

Structure Matters: Student Assessment & Reporting

1. I am indebted to Gerald Bracey for this succinct formulation of the problem. See: Gerald Bracy,, *Measurement-Driven Instruction: Catchy Phrase, Dangerous Practice,* Phi Delta Kappan, (May 1987): 683-686.

2. For a brilliant critique of our contemporary approach to teaching mathematics in schools, see "A Mathematician's Lament" by Paul Lockhart. https://www.mimuw.edu.pl/~pawelst/rzut_oka/Zajecia_dla_MISH_2011-12/Lektury_files/LockhartsLament.pdf

3. Marvin F. Wideen et al., *Impact of Large Scale Testing on the Instructional Activity of Science Teachers.* Paper presented at the Canadian Society for Studies in Education, June 1991.

4. Ibid, p. 56-57.

5. It might be objected that contemporary assessment practices—like the use of rubrics, for example—allow us to avoid these pitfalls. Not really. While the International Baccalaureate system, for example, takes great pains to separate out formative feedback (within its rubrics) from summative results, the fact remains that these "formative" assessments are eventually accumulated to yield summative scores on a 1-to-7 scale with aggregate results that inevitably represent a normal distribution curve.

6. The British philosopher Antony Flew suggested, correctly I think, that it is a measure of our "sincerity of purpose", as both teachers and learners, that

we "be concerned whether, how far, and how well [we] are succeeding, or have succeeded." Antony Flew, *Teaching and Testing,* Proceedings of the Philosophy of Education Society, (1973): 201-212.

7. For a particularly good example of a sophisticated online course, see: *The Big History Project*: https://school.bighistoryproject.com/bhplive

8. The online universe here is vast. Many major universities offer "Massive Open Online Courses"—MOOC's—that are (currently) free to the public. The revenue models for these offerings, however, are ever-changing.

9. In March 2018, it came to light that Cambridge Analytica, a political consulting firm, had accessed 50 million user profiles from Facebook to be used in the campaign to elect Donald Trump as president of the United States.

10. Quoted in: Benjamin Herold, *The Case(s) Against Personalized Learning.* Education Week, Nov 7, 2017. (accessed March 26, 2018). https://www.edweek.org/ew/articles/2017/11/08/the-cases-against-personalized-learning.html

11. https://dashboard.futurereadyschools.org/data-privacy-policy

12. In an article entitled, *Copy That: America Needs a Data Protection Law. Take Europe's and Improve On It* published April, 2018, the Economist, for example, recommends that the USA look to the General Data Protection Regulation (GDRP) as an initial template to create better data privacy regulations.

13. At a meeting of the British Columbia School Superintendents Association, for example, a representative from a local college said that their admissions people did not know how to interpret the various "student portfolios" that were coming their way.

14. http://www.coalitionforcollegeaccess.org

Structure Matters: Educational Finance

1. Jason Clemens, Joel Emes, and Deani Neven Van Pelt, *Education and Public School Enrolment in Canada, 2016 Edition.* The Fraser Institute, September 2016; Statistics Canada, *Back to School ... by the numbers. 2017* https://www.statcan.gc.ca/eng/dai/smr08/2017/smr08_220_2017#a4 ;

Statistics Canada, *Census Profile, 2016 Census, British Columbia and Canada* http://www12.statcan.gc.ca/census-recensement/2016/dp-pd/prof/details/Page.cfm?Lang=E&Geo1=PR&Code1=59&Geo2=&Code2=&Data=Count&SearchText=British%20Columbia&SearchType=Begins&SearchPR=01&B1=All&GeoLevel=PR&GeoCode=59 ;

British Columbia, Ministry of Finance, *Budget and Fiscal Plan - 2016/17 to 2018/19*; British Columbia, Ministry of Education, *Provincial Report, Students Statistics - 2016/17*, http://www.bced.gov.bc.ca/reports/pdfs/student_stats/prov.pdf

2. CBS News, *U.S. education spending tops global list, study shows.* June 25, 2013.https://www.cbsnews.com/news/us-education-spending-tops-global-list-study-shows/ ;

Investopedia, *What country spends the most on education?* https://www.investopedia.com/ask/answers/020915/what-country-spends-most-education.asp

3. The final numbers are, in fact, notoriously difficult to pinpoint. In, *The Case Against Education*, Bryan Caplan argues that the actual cost of public education in America averages to about $11,298 (US) in 2011 dollars. (Princeton University Press, 2018, p. 173) This would put its per student costs higher than Canada (i.e. factoring in the exchange), which aligns with the OECD study referred to in the previous citation.

4. Although independent schools in Canada operate apart from the public system, five out of the ten Canadian provinces provide these schools with public funding that amounts to between 35-80% of the public school per capita operating costs.

5. In the United States, 2.9 million students, or about 6% of the total student population, currently attend 7,200 charter schools. In Canada, charter schools only exist in the province of Alberta, with 13 schools located across 23 campuses.

6. Advocates of charter schools like to claim that they are held accountable for providing cost-efficient, quality education that produces the same or better results than public schools, particularly for disadvantaged students. Detractors say charter schools are not held accountable to local school boards, use selective admissions and expulsions policies, and take funding

away from traditional public schools. They also claim that charter schools do no better and often worse than traditional public schools.

7. It is important to note that many, but not all, charter schools also receive external funding via donations or private sponsorships.

8. Exceptions will arise in the salary levels paid to educational providers. In 39 states in the USA, the average teacher's salary declined relative to inflation between the 2010 and 2016 school years. (See: *A Punishing Decade for School Funding*. Michael Leachman, Kathleen Masterson, and Eric Figueroa. Center on Budget and Policy Priorities, November 29, 2017, p.10) https://www.cbpp.org/research/state-budget-and-tax/a-punishing-decade-for-school-funding

9. Joe Freedman, Charter Schools in Atlantic Canada: An Idea Whose Time Has Come, Atlantic Institute for Market Studies, http://www.aims.ca/site/media/aims/book_charter_section1.pdf ;

Possible Futures—Outlier Schools: What Can We Learn from Them?

1. The AltSchool network is a private company, while the High Tech High and Summit Schools operate as public charter schools, which means they have defined their own vision, but still get public funding. The Pacific School of Innovation and Inquiry and the Westside School in British Columbia are both independent schools, which means they get the majority of their revenue from tuition fees, with partial funding from the Ministry of Education.

2. High Tech High website: http://www.hightechhigh.org/about/index.php (March 2016)

3. See "Videos" on the High Tech High website: http://videos.hightechhigh.org/, in particular the clips entitled, "What Project Based Learning Is" and "What Project Based Learning Is Not".

4. High Tech High website: http://www.hightechhigh.org/about/ (March 2016)

5. Joanne Jacobs. *Summit Now Partnering With Over 300 Schools*. Education Next, Nov 30, 2017 http://educationnext.org/summit-now-Partnering-over-300-schools-personalized-learning/

6. Jacobs, Joanne. *Pacesetter in Personalized Learning; Summit Charter Network Shares its Model Nationwide.* Education Next, Fall, 2017, p 18. http://educationnext.org/pacesetter-in-personalized-learning-summit-charter-network-shares-model-nationwide/

7. Ibid, p. 21

8. David Osborne. The Schools of the Future: California's Summit Public Schools offer a personalized model of education that works. US News & World Report, Jan 19, 2016. https://www.usnews.com/opinion/knowledge-bank/articles/2016-01-19/californias-summit-public-schools-are-the-schools-of-the-future

9. Ibid.

10. Jacobs, Joanne. *Pacesetter in Personalized Learning; Summit Charter Network Shares its Model Nationwide.* Education Next, Fall, 2017, p 23. http://educationnext.org/pacesetter-in-personalized-learning-summit-charter-network-shares-model-nationwide/

11. Ibid, p. 24

12. Alt School website: https://www.altschool.com/about-us#about-us (March 17, 2016)

13. Mead, Rebecca. *Learn Different. Silicon Valley Disrupts Education.* New Yorker Magazine. (March 7, 2016), http://www.newyorker.com/magazine/2016/03/07/altschools-disrupted-education

14. *The PSII Approach*, PSII website, March 26, 2017. http://learningstorm.org/the-psii-approach/

15. Ibid.

16. *What's Different About PSII?* PSII website, (March 26, 2017). http://learningstorm.org/about/whats-different-about-psii/

17. It is noteworthy that one of Jeff Hopkins stated aims is to create an independent model of education using parameters that will eventually enable the public system to "put him out of business". He pays his staff, for example, full public school wages and benefits (which are roughly the

Canadian average) and is working hard to meet the ever-evolving Ministry of Education requirements, albeit by way of an unconventional roadmap.

18. The Westside Miniversity: http://www.thewestsideschools.ca/our-programs/miniversity-10-12-2/

19. Connie Loizos, *AltSchool wants to change how kids learn, but fears have surfaced that it's failing students*. TechCrunch, Nov 22, 2017. https://techcrunch.com/2017/11/22/altschool-wants-to-change-how-kids-learn-but-fears-that-its-failing-students-are-surfacing/

20. Ibid

21. Ibid

22. Quoted in: Benjamin Herold, *The Case(s) Against Personalized Learning*. Education Week, Nov 7, 2017. (accessed March 26, 2018). https://www.edweek.org/ew/articles/2017/11/08/the-cases-against-personalized-learning.html

23. Ibid

Possible Futures: Moving Forward

1. Jane. L. David. *The Who, What and Why of Site-Based Management* ASCD, Educational Leadership. December 1995/January 1996. Vol 53, No. 4, pgs 4-9 http://www.ascd.org/publications/educational_leadership/dec95/vol53/num04/The_Who,_What,_and_Why_of_Site-Based_Management.aspx

2. Jane. L David, Ibid; See also: Oliver S. Brown, *Site-Based Foolishness*. Education Week, Vol 11, Issue 19, p. 32, Jan. 29, 1991; Sharon Cromwell, *Site-Based Management: Boon or Boondoggle?* Education World, June 26, 2000.

3. Larry Kuehn, *School-based Budgeting/Site-based Management*. BCTF Research Report, Section XII, 96-EI-04

4. Jane. L David, Ibid.

5. Larry Kuehn, *School-based Budgeting/Site-based Management*. Ibid.

6. Sharon Cromwell, *Site-Based Management: Boon or Boondoggle?* Education World, June 26, 2000.
http://www.educationworld.com/a_admin/admin/admin176.shtml

7. John. H. Holloway. *The Promise and Pitfalls of Site-Based Management.* Educational Leadership, April 2000. Vol. 57, No. 7.
http://www.ascd.org/publications/educational_leadership/apr00/vol57/nu m07/_The_Promise_and_Pitfalls_of_Site-Based_Management.aspx

8. What we call "Private" schools are those that operate for profit without a governing Board. They are often international schools, language schools or trade schools (e.g., hairdressing schools) that have a single proprietor or a company as their owner. See Appendix 1 for a fuller description of types of schools.

9. That said, after each trip we made sure to have a staff debrief to review all incidents with a view to upgrading our protocols.

10. One exception, however, was when we discussed sabbatical leaves as a matter of policy because we knew this would affect the working conditions of the entire staff.

11. Schumacher, E.F., *Small is Beautiful.* London: Abacus Books, 1974, p.74

High School Reimagined: Program Elements

1. Time 4 Learning website:
https://www.time4learning.com/science.shtml
(March 2016)

2. Pearson Interactive Science Program:
http://www.pearsonschool.com/index.cfm?locator=PSZtSj (March 2016)

3. See, for example, Hyper History:
http://www.hyperhistory.com/online_n2/History_n2/a.html (March 2016)

4. See, for example, Crash Course World History:
https://www.youtube.com/playlist?list=PLBDA2E52FB1EF80C9
(March 2016)

5. We found the **Duolingo** platform to be a serviceable site for basic French practice. Teachers might also investigate the **AIM Language Learning** site as

a full-service program that takes a distinctive, and highly effective, approach to second language learning.

6. Crash Course History
https://www.youtube.com/user/crashcourse

7. We were fortunate, at Island Pacific School, to have a remarkable parent volunteer who took it upon herself to establish a robust reading culture at our school. She did this in many ways: by keeping a list of the books read by each and every student, by introducing new books and eliciting book commentaries by students during morning stretch, by arranging a reading "contest" between the houses for the most books read, and by hosting a "classics tea" for those who wanted to eat and meet together to talk about great books they had read. Her work likely reverberates through the lives of many students to this day.

8. High Tech High Projects Page:
http://www.hightechhigh.org/projects/ (March 2016)

9. Nelson, for example, has purchased a student data-tracking tool called Edusight.

Pathways for Parents

1. It is useful to remember that grade school education is compulsory, while post-secondary education (college, trades schools, university) is not. Grade school education therefore carries a deeper public responsibility. Post-secondary education is more appropriately aimed at deeper cultural studies—through the arts—and career preparation (e.g. law, science, medicine, engineering, economics, business, etc.), the pursuit of both being very much a matter of individual temperament and ability.

2. And even this does not capture the totality of what educators do. The middle school teachers at Island Pacific School, for example, teach five full academic courses, take a leadership and supervisory role in a program area (e.g., Masterworks, House System, Curriculum Coordinator, Wednesday Excursions), supervise lunch once a week, act as the Committee Chair for two Masterworks projects, participate in Wednesday excursions, attend monthly after-school staff workshops; coach ultimate and/or help out with the annual theatre production, lead and/or help supervise the Discovery Week trip and two outdoor expeditions, and complete three sets of formal report cards a year. This does not include the hours of class preparation and

marking that all teachers do. There is also the planning that individual staff put into three student exhibitions over the year (Art & Design Expo, Science Fair, and Walk Through Time), the individual meetings with students and parents, and the time spent at academic competitions and tournaments with the students, or at professional development conferences for the Staff. Although the particulars will be different, most teachers in public and other independent schools will have a roughly similar workload.

3. At Island Pacific School, we had a small cohort of "Grade Reps" that met with me about once a month to check in on how things were going and to preview upcoming initiatives. This proved to be a very effective two-way street: on one hand I could gain a better sense of what issues were of most concern to parents, while on the other hand parents could gain a bigger picture view of school operations and upcoming initiatives.

4. The *Scholastic Kids and Family Reading Report, 5th Edition* (2015). See, in particular, Section II: Reading Aloud at Home. http://www.scholastic.com/readingreport/Scholastic-KidsAndFamilyReadingReport-5thEdition.pdf

5. Ibid, p. 2

6. Alison Flood, *Only half of pre-school children being read to daily, UK study finds*. Manchester Guardian, Feb 2018. https://www.theguardian.com/books/2018/feb/21/only-half-of-pre-school-children-being-read-to-daily-study-finds

7. Common Sense Census: Media Use By Tweens and Teens https://www.commonsensemedia.org/research/the-common-sense-census-media-use-by-tweens-and-teens

Pew Research Center: *Social Media Use in 2018* http://www.pewinternet.org/2018/03/01/social-media-use-in-2018/

Kelly Wallace, *Teens spend a 'mind-boggling' 9 hours a day using media, Report says*. CNN, Nov 3, 2015. https://www.cnn.com/2015/11/03/health/teens-tweens-media-screen-use-report/index.html

Pathways for Educators

1. See, for example, Andy Hargreaves' conference presentation entitled,

Improvement, Innovation, and Inclusion: The Future of Educational Change in Ontario and Elsewhere.
https://www.youtube.com/watch?v=8JlOXeCANRc

2. First analysed formally by Clayton M. Christensen of the Harvard Business School, the basic idea of disruptive innovation is that when entrepreneurs, technologists, or visionaries figure out how to offer a product or an experience more efficiently than an incumbent company or organization—usually at a service and cost level slightly *less* than the incumbent—then they effectively *disrupt* the very manner in which this product or experience comes to be distributed. See also: Michael B. Horn & Heather Staker, *Blended: Using Disruptive Innovation to Improve Schools*, San Francisco: Jossey-Bass (Wiley Brand), 2015, p. 2-3.

3. http://www.oxfordreference.com/view/10.1093/oi/authority.20110803100229963

4. Districts that create "Demonstration Schools" can and should be upfront about what they are attempting to do and who should be involved. Parents and staff alike should be able to come to these schools voluntarily with a clear picture of what they are getting into. It is important to understand, moreover, that the core rationale for creating these schools is not to provide greater *choice* for students and families, but instead to improve the *quality* of the educational experience for all students.

Appendix 1

1. Angela MacLeod and Said Hasan, Where are Students are Educated: Measuring Student Enrolment in Canada - 2017, Fraser Institute
www.fraserinstitute.org/studies/where-our-students-are-educated-measuring-student-enrolment-in-canada-2017

Maureen Boland, School types: The difference between public, private, magnet, charter, and more, Sept 2016
https://www.babycenter.com/0_school-types-the-difference-between-public-private-magnet-ch_67288.bc ,

Our Kids (website), Why do parents consider private schooling?

http://www.ourkids.net/school/about-private-schools.php

Council for American Private Education, Facts and Studies, www.capenet.org/facts.html

Sarah Grady, A Fresh Look at Homeschooling in the USA, National Center for Education Statistics, Sept 26, 2017. https://nces.ed.gov/blogs/nces/post/a-fresh-look-at-homeschooling-in-the-u-s

2. Canadian Accredited Independent Schools www.cais.ca
National Association of Independent Schools www.nais.org
National Independent Private Schools Association www.nipsa.org

Appendix 1

Types of Schools[1]

There are essentially three ways to educate children in Canada and the United States: public schools, private schools (including independent schools), and homeschooling.

Public Schools

Public schools get most, or all, of their funding from local, state or provincial, and federal sources (e.g., taxes). They do not charge tuition fees (although some charge extra program fees). They typically admit all students who live within the borders of their districts.

Public schools come in many forms:

- Neighbourhood schools (operated by state departments or provincial ministries of Education)
- Magnet schools, or Academies, that offer specialized programs, e.g., arts, sciences, sports (also operated by state departments or provincial ministries of Education)
- Charter schools that are publicly-funded and do not charge tuition fees but are operated by independent bodies (e.g., charter management organizations, corporations). These are far more prevalent in the United States than Canada.

In Canada, there are also "separate"—but publicly funded—school systems for religious denominations in three provinces: Alberta, Saskatchewan, and

Ontario. There are also publicly-funded Francophone schools in all provinces, with Quebec and New Brunswick having the largest number of these. There is little to no public funding for denominational or culture-based schools in the United States.

Private (and Independent) Schools

Private schools are funded by way of tuition fees and other non-public sources such as religious organizations, endowments, grants, and charitable donations. They typically accept students on the basis of specified admissions policies.

They too come in many shapes and sizes:

- Religious schools
- Special focus schools (e.g., Montessori, special needs schools)
- University prep schools (including independent schools)
- Proprietary schools (i.e., for-profit, privately owned and operated schools)

Independent schools are typically non-profit organizations operated by a Board of Governors with an arm's length relationship to the principal or head of school. Many, but not all, independent schools have a university preparatory orientation and are accredited by a national body—the Canadian Accredited Independent Schools (CAIS) in Canada and the National Association of Independent Schools (NAIS) in the USA. In British Columbia, however, all non-government schools are called "independent" schools.[2]

Religious schools, as a category, make up the largest percentage of private schools in Canada and the United States: 48% in Canada and 70% in America. The apparent gap in attendance at religious schools closes somewhat when you consider that, in Canada, some students have the option of attending religious schools within the *public* system.

Home Schooling

Home schooling is typically defined as the education of children at home by their parents. Home school families, however, also make use of tutors, parent cooperatives, and—more recently—online programs. (The increase in "distributed learning" resources is becoming increasingly popular for homeschoolers.) At least one public school district in British Columbia currently offers a hybrid arrangement where students come to a learning center for 2-3 days/week and use the remaining days of the week to learn at home.

At present, about 1.5% of the students in Canada and 3.3% of the students in the USA are homeschoolers. There is conflicting data as to whether these percentages are increasing or have become stabilized at their current rates.

Appendix 2

List of IPS Masterworks Presentations

1995-2019

The following is an abbreviated list of Masterworks projects completed at Island Pacific School between 1995-2019. Here is what happens when you ask 14-year-old students what they are interested in:

- The Art of Knife Making
- An Historical & Contemporary Analysis of Counter-Terrorism Units
- A Contemporary Examination of Multiple Personality Disorder
- Black Holes: The Beginning of the End?
- Two Way Language Communication Between Humans and Apes
- The Truth is Out There: An Introduction to UFOlogy
- Roller Coasters: The Anatomy of Fear
- Freud & Psychoanalysis
- An Introductory Examination of Judaism and Christianity
- The Underground Railway
- A Life of Sarah Bernhardt
- An Analysis of Violence, Poverty, and Socio-Cultural Responsibility
- Team New Zealand: Defending the America's Cup
- A Voyage of Faith (St. Brendan)
- Buddhism: A Cultural Study
- An Analysis of Social Morality in Modern Society with Reference to Lawrence Kohlberg
- Britannia Mine: An Environmental Issue

- Power to the People: A Look at Anarchy and Its Implications in Our Lives
- Mission Impossible: Preventing the Rwandan Genocide
- Haunted Heroes: The Reason for Military Ethics
- Genetically Engineered Food
- Natural Horsemanship
- Mount Everest: The People, The Risk, The Impact
- Cloning: Designing a Brave New World or Designing Disaster?
- The Legalization of Marijuana: An Exploration of the Issues
- Cults: With an Emphasis on the Jonestown Tragedy
- Pain: The Two Sides
- The Australian Aboriginals' Story: A Lesson for our Planet
- Different Beliefs on What Happens When We Die
- Clinical Depression: An Analysis of an Ailment
- Astrobiology: Understanding the Potential for Life on Other Planets
- Feng Shui: The Chinese Art of Placement
- Ernest Shackleton and the Essence of Great Leadership
- A Philosophical Look at the Animal Rights Movement
- Intelligent Design: The Scientific Case for Intelligent Design in our Universe
- Secret Societies
- Fashion Through the Ages and Its Effects on Women's Rights
- Can We Justify Zoos?
- The Science of Time
- The Search for Grand Unified Theories
- Voodoo
- Sound Versus Silence: An Overview of Cochlear Implants
- Drama as a Reflection of Social and Political Climate
- Terraforming Mars
- Nimue: An Examination of the Writing Process
- The Many Worlds Interpretation in Quantum Mechanics
- Frogs as a Canary Species
- The Meaning of Life
- The Gaia Hypothesis

- The Weight of You (A One-Act Play)
- Teenage Depression
- Cold Fusion: The Other-Other Nuclear Power
- Go Lemmings Go! Media and Advertising and Their Effect on Consumerism in Society
- The Pressure to Be Perfect: An Examination of Western Society's Approach to Body Image
- Bully: The Causes and Effects of Relational Aggression
- Spooky Action at a Distance: Entanglement and Its Applications
- Air Pollution and Climate Change: A Study of Vehicular Emissions
- Eating Disorders: Dying to Be Thin
- Shucks: Design and Format of a Successful Oyster Bar
- Creating a Profitable Water Park
- Is Dyslexia a Learning Disability or Do Teachers Have a Teaching Disability?
- The Physics of Flight
- The Eco House
- In Your Dreams: The Importance of Dreams Through the Ages
- The Ethics of Stem Cell Research
- A Brief History of Boat Building & The Process of Building a Boat
- Why Should We Care About Garbage?
- Why, and How, Do Human Beings Develop Phobias? A Day in the Life of a Phobic Person
- What Can Be Learned From Past Life Regression Therapy?
- What Physical and Mental Attributes Does It Take To Survive in the Wilderness for Five Days?
- How Can I Create a Video Game?
- Micro Hydro: A Journey From Rushing River to Running Lights
- The Possibility of Perpetual Motion
- Composition in Wonderland: A Creative Exploration of Three Different Musical Composers' Styles
- Shades of Grey: Creating Social Change Through Photography
- The Beautiful Game: The Sport That Changes Lives
- Exploring the Existence of Fate in the Stars

- Under Pressure: The Life and Pressure of an Elite Athlete
- Playing the Part: An In-Depth Study of Acting Techniques
- The Effects of Recording Techniques on the Sound of a Song
- Remixing the Moonwalk: Teaching the School to Dance Like the King of Pop
- The Making of *Between the Lines* (Student Film)
- Refugees of Rwanda: My Journey to the Heart of Africa to Meet Youth Displaced by War
- Codes and Ciphers
- Still Movement: A Study in Capturing Movement Through Still Photography
- Bebo's Kitchen Memories: The Process of Creating and Publishing a Cookbook
- The Vancouver Marine Mammal Rescue Program
- How Yoga Assists Football Players Both Mentally and Physically
- Manga for the Masses. The Making of a Webcomic
- My Journey into the Land of Programming
- A Dancer's Journey: An Investigation Into the Making of a Successful Dancer
- Don't Worry, Be Happy - A Study in the Science of Happiness
- Forging a Fantasy Sword
- Building a Bike Frame
- Sweet or Sour: A Look Into How Sugar is Rapidly Changing our Diet
- Building a Community Bike Park
- Concept to Product: Designing a Backpack
- Writing a Novella
- Designing and Creating a Clothing Line
- Becoming an Entrepreneur
- Designing and Shaping a Surfboard
- Fly Fishing - Steps to Success
- Climate Change in British Columbia
- Car Design – Then and Now
- Through the Lens - A Guide to Action Cinematography
- Growing North - Food Security in the Arctic

- How are Music and Emotion Connected?
- Fusion: Energy of the Future
- ADHD From My Point of View
- The Sound of Music: An In-Depth Look into the Physics of Sound
- Building a Ukulele
- The Art of Special Effects
- How Geography Affects Music
- Attachment - In theory and Practice in a Ghanaian Orphanage
- Architecture: A Study of Environmentally Friendly Residential Structures
- Making the Perfect Shred Sticks: A Look Into Manufacturing a Pair of Skis
- An Investigation into the Effects of Electromagnetic Radiation
- Purple: The Process of Telling Someone's Story
- From Road Bike to Racer- Customizing a GL500
- The Culture and History of Skateboarding
- The Effects of Captivity on Dolphins
- Sports Analytics; Changing the Game
- From Dream to Screen: The Process of Writing a Screenplay
- Dancing through the Decades: Women's Roles in Society Reflected in Dance
- The End of the Universe as We Know It
- Expressive Art Therapy
- Fantasy on High: An Anthology of Short Stories
- Video Games- A look at the Coding Behind Your Favourite Pastime
- Jazz Music and Black Rights - Evolving Together in America
- 'Playing God' - the Ethics, Science and Legality of Gene Editing
- What is the Meaning Behind our Dreams? A Cultural and Historical look at Dream Analysis
- Social Engineering: The Psychological Methods Hackers use to Steal your Information
- Games, Fame and the Victorious Claim: An In-Depth Analysis of Why We Play Games
- Anxiety Disorders - Methods of Coping

- The Basics of Film Acting
- Mechanical Engineering of High-End Bicycles
- Plastic Pollution in our Oceans
- Are Ghosts Real? - A Study of the Paranormal
- My Journey through Animation
- Make-up Effects: Transformation for Film and Television

Appendix 3

A "Parent Orientation" Note to Parents

Pebbles in a Pond: The Point & Purpose of Island Pacific School
Ted Spear, Ph.D.
Island Pacific School Parent Orientation
September 13, 2016

Before I get into some particulars and highlights about the school year, I wonder if you would indulge me for just a few minutes to let me explain, one more time, what Island Pacific School is really all about.

Island Pacific School is a member of the Independent Schools Association of BC (ISABC). These are the so-called "high end" schools in British Columbia, of which IPS is definitely the smallest. ISABC schools like to present and define themselves as "University Prep Schools." Because we are a middle school, some people sometimes get the idea that what we are essentially all about is giving students a strong academic foundation so that they can do well in high school and go on to university. I would say to those people that while this is certainly part of the equation, it is not the whole thing and, in fact, it is not the most important thing in what we do.

Now, don't get me wrong: I want our kids to do well in the world as it is, so part of our job is indeed to give them a strong foundation in these middle schools so that they can acquit themselves well in the next chapter of their education. Jennifer Henrichsen works very hard to make sure our students don't crash and burn in Math 10, and all of the staff, especially myself, are determined that they will learn how to write reasonably coherently. But while this is indeed part of what we do, it does not completely capture what we are really trying to pull off.

To explain this, I need you to understand something that has been bugging me through 20 years of education: in looking at the ways that schools operate—even Island Pacific School on a bad day—I can't get over my suspicion that what we are offering is little more than a cheap facsimile of what a genuine education could and should be.

In the broadest possible terms, I think that the true function of education—and I know I have said this before—is to equip and inspire students to cultivate their humanity.

The term "cultivate humanity" refers back to the classical ideal of a liberal education which proposes that in order for a person to be truly free, they need to develop and express their distinctly human capacities: i.e., their capacity to reason, to be creative, to be physically intentional, to be compassionate, and to be moral agents that act on principle.

If this is the goal, then the job of schools is to "equip and inspire" students toward that end, i.e., give them the tools and experiences they need to express the very best of who they are.

So what does this have to do with the kind of middle school education we want to give our kids at Island Pacific School? Just this: in addition to preparing kids for high school and university, what we are really all about is creating the conditions to make two kinds of overlapping invitations to our kids.

We want to make an intellectual invitation whereby we initiate students into the great conversations of human inquiry. In the achievements of science, math, art, humanities, literature, and philosophy, human beings have had these ongoing conversations that we want to draw our students into. Sometimes it happens in Pam's science classes when she ignites the spark of scientific inquiry, and sometimes it happens in Adrian's classes when he asks challenging questions about democracy, nationalism, and imperialism.

But we also want to extend a personal invitation to our students to begin the journey, in these adolescent years, of defining who they are. At Island Pacific School, we set before our students a series of challenges. There are, firstly, the challenges of the outdoor trips, the clean-up supervision, Mainstage participation, Ultimate, fitness, and Masterworks. And there are also the personal challenges to our students: for example, to do the right thing in shutting down negative gossip and take direct responsibility for a transgression.

Both these invitations are meant to be like pebbles dropped into a pond, with ripples that can potentially extend across a lifetime.

Another way to explain this is to say that what we are really after are a very precise set of residual effects. At a staff orientation in August, we once introduced the metaphor of our school as a bubbling cauldron: there is a lot of action and energy at the school all year long, but what we want to remain at the end of the day is a particular kind of residue. In academics, students will likely not remember the parts of the cell, or the conjugation of all the irregular verbs, or even types of claims in Practical Reasoning, but they may eventually get a sense of the beauty of science, the power of having a second language, and the importance of reasons. In terms of personal growth, they may forget all the lines to their play, but remember that they had the courage to stand on stage; or, they may forget the stupid little thing they did that got them in trouble but remember vividly how good they felt in dealing with it in a forthright manner.

The goal of Island Pacific School, therefore, is to expose our kids to a whirlwind of knowledge and experience in the hope they will take up those invitations along the way and so gain those residual effects that will eventually allow them to express the very best of who they are.

We want our kids, in other words, to not only "do well" in the world as it is, but to "be well" in the world as it could be.

This is a monumental goal, so it is important to understand that we are not always going to hit the mark. On a normal or mediocre day at IPS, we are going to be just a "school." We will be running kids through the MYP and BC Curriculum; we will be talking to kids rather than talking with them; we will be simply occupying their time over a course of a day, as opposed to engaging them. Given the teaching line-up that we have this year, I hope and trust that we do not have too many of those days.

On a good or exceptional day, however, we are going to be a place where the invitation is accepted, i.e., where the pebble is thrown into the pond; where a personal challenge is confronted; where curiosity, or courage, or integrity or compassion are engaged; where a kid takes one small step forward in learning to express the very best of who they are—who we are.

And interestingly enough, of course, what is going to be a "normal" day for one kid will be an exceptional day for another.

And while there will be day-to-day fluctuations back and forth, what we are really after over the four years at Island Pacific School is a cumulative effect that ends up creating an exceptional and remarkable middle school experience for our students.

The motto at Island Pacific School is "wisdom, courage, integrity." Those are big words and big aspirations. In trying to explain to 11- to 14-year-old students what we mean by them, we tell the students that what we essentially want to happen for them is that when they leave, we want people to point to them and say, "There goes a kid with a head on his or her shoulders!"
And then we explain that what we want those people to mean by that is at least three things:

- We want them to be recognized as kids who are reasonably knowledgeable about the world—that is, that they are not breathtakingly ignorant about things. This is the beginning of wisdom, for wisdom consists not only of having knowledge but also of knowing how and when to use it.

- We want them to be recognized as kids who have a certain kind of confidence. Not arrogance but instead an earned confidence that comes from having accepted a range of challenges—academic, physical, social—that give them the kind of courage to try new things.

We want them to be recognized as kids who are basically good human beings. We sometimes say to our kids, "We do not want you to be the kind of people who throw rocks at little old ladies." That is a simple proxy, of course, for the much deeper idea that we want them to be the kind of people who take responsibility for themselves and, therefore, the kind of people who end up becoming part of the solution rather than part of the problem. We want them, in other words, to become persons of integrity.

So, yes, part of the purpose of Island Pacific School is to prepare our students for high school and university. But the more fundamental purpose is to create a middle-years experience that will significantly impact who they become for the rest of their lives.

This is the heart of the matter. This is why Adrian, Jennifer, Pam, Victoria, Barb, Amanda, Diana, and Jen have worked so hard over the past years at IPS, and why we were happy to have Charlotte, Laura, and Stuart join us this year.

We have an enormous job to do at the school which we will strive to get right as much as is humanly possible. Our most important partners in all of this are, of course, the parents. Your goodwill and support in helping us pursue this shared goal will be not only appreciated but in fact central to our essential project.

Speaking personally—and perhaps even a bit selfishly—I am hoping that we can keep these core purposes firmly rooted in our minds because, if we do, we have a chance to make 2016-17 the best year ever at Island Pacific School. My thanks, then, for your help with that.

Appendix 4

A Few Important Books & Resources

There have been literally thousands of books written and online resources created that address the purposes and practices of education. These typically fall into a number of category types with different readers in mind. Here are just a few examples of some pivotal books and online resources that point to a different way to think about education and schools.

The End of Average by Todd Rose (Harper Collins, 2016)

This is a "big ideas" book that details how our fixation with identifying scaled performance has significantly undermined individual potential. This is a must read for parents and educators who are looking for a better way to approach the whole universe of student achievement.

Deep Learning: Engage the World Change the World by Michael Fullan (Corwin Press, 2018)

A good example of how a highly-regarded professional educator who has spent a career studying schools has reimagined the next generation of schools. An important and necessary read for ambitious teachers and educational administrators looking to make system-wide change.

Blended: Using Disruptive Innovation to Improve Schools **by Michael B. Horn & Heather Staker (Jossey-Bass, 2015)**

The baseline textbook that enables educational practitioners to understand (and implement) "Blended Learning" strategies as an expression of disruptive innovation. Although aimed at teachers and administrators, parents would benefit by reading this book, if only to gain a better understanding of the potential and pitfalls of newly-emerging teaching strategies.

The Schools Our Children Deserve **by Alfie Kohn (Houghton Mifflin, 1999)**

Alfie Kohn is a powerful and prolific writer on the state of contemporary education. He has written at least 15 books on K-12 schooling, any one of which offers insightful critiques—and common-sense solutions—to the multiple shortcomings of our schools. His books are informative and accessible to parents and educators alike.

The Case Against Education: Why the Education System is a Waste of Time and Money **by Bryan Caplan (Princeton University Press, 2018)**

A high-level read written by a university economist that offers some disturbing (but true) observations about our contemporary school system. Although I disagree with his conclusions, the questions he raises are more than worthy of our attention. Despite his pessimism about the "value" of contemporary education, I think he gives us an opening for a third way forward. Let the conversation continue!

Big History Project **by David Christian**

An online course that takes full advantage of mixed media resources to create a remarkably comprehensive and multi-layered learning experience for students. This is a good example of the kinds of online courses that will likely become a key element in the next generation of schools. This one is worth a look.

The Khan Academy by Sal Khan

If you have not yet visited the Khan Academy, the time has come. This is an online learning site that offers computer-aided instruction in a variety of school subjects. The platform offers a good example of the basic online learning architecture that is being replicated on many other sites across the internet. There are different entry portals for "teachers," "students," and "parents," so exploring all three will give you a good idea of how these kids of resources are meant to be utilized by multiple users.

The Glossary of Educational Reform by the Great Schools Partnership

A comprehensive online resource that enable parents and educators alike to search for intelligible explanations of much used—but little-understood—education terms. A quick way to cut through the jargon to get to the meat of the issues at hand. Locates each explanation within the larger context of education reform and offers a fairly comprehensive sense of the current debate around the concept in question. An invaluable resource for parents, in particular, to make better sense of the changing educational landscape.

About the Author

Ted Spear has worked for over 25 years as a teacher and administrator in public and independent schools. His career has expressed a lifelong fascination with the purpose and practices of K-12 education. After completing a Ph.D. in Education, he and a small group of dedicated teachers and parents founded Island Pacific School, an independent middle school in British Columbia. It is there that he discovered what matters most in creating a powerful education for young people. He also served as a middle school principal at a K-12 school in Vancouver, and co-founded another high school on Vancouver Island. He now lives on Bowen Island, British Columbia.

To learn more, visit www.tedspear.com

Island Pacific School ~ Bowen Island, BC